Hegemony & History

Alongside Herbert Butterfield, Martin Wight and Hedley Bull, Adam Watson was a member of the British Committee on the Theory of International Politics and a founding member of the English School. The committee sought to explore relations between states in an historical context and developed a theory of international society and the nature of order in world politics. These theories have had an important impact on the discipline of international relations, providing a framework and research agenda for understanding international politics that continues to shape the discipline in the present day.

This fascinating collection traces the development of Watson's thinking on international theory and politics from the 1950s to the present. Its primary focus is on how present and past hegemonial systems function. The quest also led him to explore a range of topical issues including:

- The behaviour of states in international systems and societies
- Justice
- Non-state relations, including the economic involvement of communities and the role of other non-state actors
- Aid and intervention
- The increasing focus of international politics on individuals as well as states

This book will be of strong interest to students and researchers of international relations, political science, history and economics, as well as diplomatic practitioners and others concerned with international affairs.

Adam Watson, diplomat and historian, has published several books on historical and international subjects; including *The Limits of Independence; The Evolution of International Society* and a study of the Muslim conquest of South India. After 30 years in the British Diplomatic Service, culminating with service as Ambassador and Assistant Under-Secretary of State, he directed two Swiss human rights foundations. Since 1978 he has been a Professor of International Relations at the University of Virginia.

The New International Relations
Edited by Barry Buzan, *London School of Economics* and Richard Little, *University of Bristol*

The field of international relations has changed dramatically in recent years. This new series will cover the major issues that have emerged and reflect the latest academic thinking in this particular dynamic area.

International Law, Rights and Politics
Developments in Eastern Europe and the CIS
Rein Mullerson

The Logic of Internationalism
Coercion and accommodation
Kjell Goldmann

Russia and the Idea of Europe
A study in identity and international relations
Iver B. Neumann

The Future of International Relations
Masters in the making?
Edited by *Iver B. Neumann and Ole Wæver*

Constructing the World Polity
Essays on international institutionalization
John Gerard Ruggie

Realism in International Relations and International Political Economy
The continuing story of a death foretold
Stefano Guzzini

International Relations, Political Theory and the Problem of Order
Beyond international relations theory?
N.J. Rengger

War, Peace and World Orders in European History
Edited by *Anja V. Hartmann and Beatrice Heuser*

European Integration and National Identity
The challenge of the Nordic states
Edited by *Lene Hansen and Ole Wæver*

Shadow Globalization, Ethnic Conflicts and New Wars
A political economy of intra-state war
Dietrich Jung

Contemporary Security Analysis and Copenhagen Peace Research
Edited by *Stefano Guzzini and Dietrich Jung*

Observing International Relations
Niklas Luhmann and world politics
Edited by *Mathias Albert and Lena Hilkermeier*

Does China Matter? A Reassessment
Essays in memory of Gerald Segal
Edited by Barry Buzan and Rosemary Foot

European Approaches to International Relations Theory
A house with many mansions
Jörg Friedrichs

The Post-Cold War International System
Strategies, institutions and reflexivity
Ewan Harrison

States of Political Discourse
Words, regimes, seditions
Costas M. Constantinou

The Politics of Regional Identity
Meddling with the Mediterranean
Michelle Pace

The Power of International Theory
Reforging the link to foreign policy-making through scientific enquiry
Fred Chernoff

Africa and the North
Between globalization and marginalization
Edited by Ulf Engel and Gorm Rye Olsen

Communitarian International Relations
The epistemic foundations of international relations
Emanuel Adler

Human Rights and World Trade
Hunger in international society
Ana Gonzalez-Pelaez

Liberalism and War
The victors and the vanquished
Andrew Williams

Constructivism and International Relations
Alexander Wendt and his critics
Edited by Stefano Guzzini and Anna Leander

Security as Practice
Discourse analysis and the Bosnian war
Lene Hansen

The Politics of Insecurity
Fear, migration and asylum in the EU
Jef Huysmans

State Sovereignty and Intervention
A discourse analysis of interventionary and non-interventionary practices in Kosovo and Algeria
Helle Malmvig

Culture and Security
Symbolic power and the politics of international security
Michael Williams

Hegemony & History
Adam Watson

Hegemony & History

Adam Watson

Routledge
Taylor & Francis Group
LONDON AND NEW YORK

First published 2007
by Routledge
2 Park Square, Milton Park, Abingdon, Oxon, OX14 4RN

Simultaneously published in the USA and Canada
by Routledge
270 Madison Avenue, New York, NY 10016

Routledge is an imprint of the Taylor & Francis Group, an informa business

Transferred to Digital Printing 2007

© 2007 Adam Watson

Typeset in Sabon
by Keystroke, 28 High Street, Tettenhall, Wolverhampton

All rights reserved. No part of this book may be reprinted or reproduced or utilized in any form or by any electronic, mechanical, or other means, now known or hereafter invented, including photocopying and recording, or in any information storage or retrieval system, without permission in writing from the publishers.

British Library Cataloguing in Publication Data
A catalogue record for this book is available from the British Library

Library of Congress Cataloging in Publication Data
Watson, Adam, 1914–
Hegemony & history / Adam Watson.
p. cm. – (The new international relations)
Includes bibliographical references and index.
ISBN 0–415–39343–4 (hardback : alk. paper) 1. Hegemony.
2. International relations. I. Title.
JZ1312.W38 2007
327.101–dc22
2006018426

ISBN10: 0–415–39343–4 (hbk)
ISBN10: 0–415–43232–4 (pbk)

ISBN13: 978–0–415–39343–0 (hbk)
ISBN13: 978–0–415–43232–0 (pbk)

To Barry Buzan and Richard Little who have taken a long way further the exploration described in this book and to Brunello Vigezzi who has successfully shone the light of history on the achievements and potential of the British Committee for the Theory of International Politics where the exploration began.

Then felt I like some watcher of the skies
When a new planet swims into his ken;
Or like stout Cortez, when with eagle eyes
He stared at the Pacific—and all his men
Looked at each other with a wild surmise—
Silent upon a peak in Darien
                              John Keats
      On First Looking into Chapman's Homer

Contents

Series editors' preface		xi
Author's introductory note		xiv
Acknowledgements		xv
1	Introduction: A voyage of exploration	1
2	The British Committee on the Theory of International Politics	10
3	Martin Wight and the Theory of International Relations	14
4	Hedley Bull, states systems and international societies	27
5	The Anarchical Society in the history of international relations: Discussions with Hedley Bull	35
6	Justice between states	38
7	The prospects for a more integrated international society	46
8	"The Practice Outruns the Theory"	54
9	The future of the Westphalian anti-hegemonial international system	64
10	International relations and the practice of hegemony	80
11	The changing international system	92
12	1878: A case study in collective hegemony	98
13	Hegemony & History	103
	Bibliography	115
	Index	118

Series editors' preface

Hegemony has been a central concept in mainstream thinking about international relations for more than two decades, although the evaluation of the concept has changed dramatically over that period. In the 1980s, the theoretical focus of interest was on how to maintain regimes in the face of the declining hegemonic influence of the United States. The dominant image at that time was of the United States operating as a benign hegemon, willing and able to establish and maintain a rule governed order in the first world. But it was also widely assumed in the 1980s that the balance of power was shifting in the West and that Europe and Japan were starting to challenge US hegemony. What would the world look like, after hegemony? With the ending of the Cold War and the demise of the Soviet Union this question was, of course, soon considered to be redundant and the interest of theorists re-focused on the world-wide implications of unipolarity and the putative emergence of the United States as a global hegemon. With the new millennium, when it began to appear as if the United States was moving in an increasingly unilateralist direction, the preoccupation with hegemony in the study of international relations expanded. Much of this debate shifted terms into the ongoing debate about whether the United States should be seen as an empire or not, and whether or not such a shift was desirable.

Adam Watson's preoccupation with hegemony and empire, however, goes back much further than the 1980s and from the start he viewed these concepts from a world historical perspective, seeing developments in the second half of the twentieth century as part of a process that can be traced back for at least five thousand years. This book sheds significant light on this process; but, in doing so, also provides a fascinating record of an intellectual journey by a very remarkable man. The journey is inseparable from the history of the British Committee on the Theory of International Politics, the precursor of the English School approach to international relations, and so this book provides, incidentally, new insights on how this school of thought evolved. Both the structure of the debates in the British Committee, and Watson's role in them, have been made available in Brunello Vigezzi's recent book, and the two books can usefully be read in conjunction for insight into how and why the English School began. Having these insights into the foundational debates provides a useful benchmark both for where we are now, and what puzzles and issues have endured. Watson admits quite frankly that the British Committee started with a state-centric bias and a preoccupation with what Hedley Bull identified as a pluralist approach to international relations. As a consequence, the members of the Committee were not only interested in how a system of independent sovereign states has been, and can be, maintained, but they also highlighted that, despite all its flaws, such a system is preferable to any practical alternative.

But Watson was never predisposed to accept a possible corollary of pluralism, that there is no need to investigate historical international systems that fail to display pluralist characteristics. Unlike so much of modern international relations theory, which sees the world through the lenses of post-Westphalian European history, Watson was convinced that to develop a plausible and useful theory of international relations it is essential to examine the complete range of international systems. It was this conviction that generated both *The Evolution of International Society* (1992), his magisterial extension of Wight's studies of premodern international societies, and his pendulum model of international systems. This model envisages the history of international relations in terms of a pendulum swinging across a continuum that stretches from world government ('empire' in Watson's terms) at one extreme to unconstrained anarchy at the other, with dominion, suzerainty and hegemony in between. Watson concluded from his study of world history that although the pendulum does swing across the continuum, there is an historical tendency for the pendulum to pull away from both world government and anarchy towards hegemony. From Watson's perspective, then, the hegemony displayed by the United States in the contemporary international system is not the exception, but closer to the rule in international relations. Watson's pendulum theory, and particularly its distinctions along the way between anarchy and empire, could usefully be read by many current pundits who rush too quickly to talk about empire without really understanding either the dynamics of the pendulum or the independent importance of hegemony in anarchic international systems.

It would be a mistake to infer from the pendulum model that Watson subscribes to a mechanistic view of history, with states participating in endless and unchanging cycles of behaviour. He is, in fact, acutely sensitive to the large number of factors that differentiate one international system from another. By the same token, he is also fully aware that the British Committee's view of international relations was restricted and he fully recognizes the need to take more account of economics (although he argues that the founding fathers were more aware of this factor than is often recognized) and non-state actors. He also recognizes the limitations of some of the most familiar theoretical tools employed by members of the British Committee. His comments on the well-known distinction that Bull draws between international systems and international societies are particularly astute, recognizing the problematic nature of the distinction but remaining convinced that it is impossible to manage without it. From Watson's perspective, however, there is no doubt that the distinction needs more theoretical consideration, and it is partly through his questioning that this issue remains a hot topic within English School theory debates. We do not agree as yet on the best way to handle this issue, and will need in the future to draw on and extend the debate about the distinction that Adam Watson started with Hedley Bull in the 1970s.

By a happy coincidence, Adam Watson's book is the last that we will cooperate on as joint editors of this series, and that is partly why we deviate from our usual practice and offer a jointly written preface. Barry Buzan is withdrawing as an editor because of other commitments. He is being replaced by Iver Neumann and Jutta Weldes. As the two of us, and many others in our cohort, edge ever closer to retirement, Adam Watson acts as a wonderful if rather daunting role model. He retired, after an extraordinarily full and fulfilled career as a diplomat in 1968, and the very significant contribution that he has made to the field of international relations theory has been carried out primarily during the course of his second career as an academic. Adam Watson is a living embodiment of the original wisdom of the British Committee in bringing together academics and practitioners to think big about international relations. The wisdom of making this combination remains, but making it happen has become much more difficult, and for better or worse the English School is now almost exclusively an academic enterprise. We are delighted that he has placed his latest book in our series.

Barry Buzan and Richard Little

Author's introductory note

The purpose of this book is to make available in one volume a selection of statements, published and unpublished, which record the development of my thinking about international theory from the 1950s to the present. I hope that academics and students in faculties of political science and related subjects like history and economics, and also diplomatic practitioners and others concerned with international affairs, will be interested. My publications and discussions on the evolution of international theory have formed part of the English School and illustrate its development from its limited beginnings in the British Committee on the Theory of International Politics 50 years ago. I am almost the sole survivor of the whole voyage of exploration. It seems to me that an effective illustration needs to present the stages of development together in sequence. Hitherto the published documents have no doubt been available to serious researchers but not together in the reader's hand; and the unpublished ones have not been available elsewhere.

Adam Watson,
Charlottesville, VA
March 2006

Acknowledgements

The author and publishers would like to thank the following for granting permission to reproduce material in this work:

- Blackwell Publishing, Oxford, UK for granting permission to reproduce the following: Adam Watson, "The British Committee on the Theory of International Politics," *Review of International Studies* 27, 3, July 2001; Adam Watson, "Hedley Bull, States Systems and International Societies," *Review of International Studies* 13, 2, April 1987: 147–53.
- Continuum International Publishing Group, London, UK for granting permission to reproduce: Adam Watson, "The Practice Outruns the Theory" *International Society and the Development of International Relations Theory* ed. B. A. Roberson (London: Continuum, 1998).
- Sage Publications India, New Dehli, India for granting permission to reproduce: Adam Watson, "The Prospects for a More Integrated International Society," reproduced from Kanti BAJPAI and Harish C SHUKUL(eds): *Interpreting World Politics: Essays for A.P. Rana.* Copyright © Kanti BAJPAI and Harish C SHUKUL, 1995. All rights reserved. Reproduced with the permission of the copyright holders and the publishers, Sage Publications India Pvt. Ltd., New Delhi, India.

Every effort has been made to contact copyright holders for their permission to reprint material in this book. The publishers would be grateful to hear from any copyright holder who is not here acknowledged and will undertake to rectify any errors or omissions in future editions of this book.

1 Introduction: A voyage of exploration

This record of my voyage of exploration into the uncharted realms of international relations theory begins with the wholly state-centred investigations of the British Committee on the Theory of International Politics[1] into systems and societies of states, and my sense of the need to study past systems, each in their own individuality, and then compare them with the present one. It continues with my deduction that the systems for which we have evidence arrange themselves in a spectrum between the theoretical extremes of total independent anarchy and total world government; and my study of the role of hegemony in the anarchic half of the spectrum. Later chapters illustrate my growing sense of the importance of non-state relations, including the economic involvement of communities and the role of other non-state actors; and arising out of this extended picture, my awareness of the increasing focus of international politics on individuals as well as states.

My voyage of exploration effectively began with the work of the British Committee. Chapter 2 serves as a summary of the Committee's achievements, and as an indication of the need to continue where the Committee left off. The research and theorizing has now broadened out into what is known as the English School: a diverse array of scholars and thinkers. Much of the present work of the English School pivots round the collaborative contribution of Barry Buzan and Richard Little.

Chapter 3, entitled Martin Wight and the Theory of International Relations, describes my relation to the way Wight and the other members of the British Committee saw its task. It was Wight who launched the intellectual journey with his seminal essay "Why is there no International Theory?"[2] International Politics meant for us the political and strategic relations between independent states, or more specifically between the executive branches of their governments, locked in a system. Most of us looked at these relations in an historical context. The four determining members of the original Committee, Butterfield, Wight, Howard and Williams, were all historians. They saw the need to step outside the academic world to bring in diplomatic practitioners with historical training and interests, such as myself, and later Robert Wade-Gery from the British Foreign Office and Noel Dorr from the Irish Ministry for Foreign Affairs.

2 Introduction: A voyage of exploration

The Committee's concentration on the behaviour of states in international systems and societies was reasonable enough. There was no adequate theory even of that, and one was sorely needed. But as we looked at the patterns, we became aware how much the rules and codes of conduct of states in international societies were also shaped by two motive forces: first, inter-state economic activity; and second, a sense of cultural and ethical responsibilities that was non-governmental and derived from individuals, including statesmen acting as individuals. At first, we were only dimly aware of the vast extent of the problem and its inescapability for any comprehensive theory of international relations. We were like Keats's Cortez and his men staring at the unforeseen Pacific "with a wild surmise." But gradually, as the outlines of this new continent, so to speak, became clearer to us, we began to ask ourselves the relevant questions and to feel our way towards answers.

From the beginning, the Committee was concerned with the ethical or moral dimension of the relations between states. Butterfield and Wight held that coercion and other forms of naked pressure by some states on others, such as might occur in conditions of anarchy, were mitigated in an international society, and especially in the European one: not so much by unenforceable international law as by the restraints of prudence and moral obligation. Prudence was a matter of calculation, enshrined in maxims of statecraft like "the enemy of today will be needed as an ally tomorrow." But moral obligation was rather a matter of belief, a set of values distilled from the common culture of the member states. In the European case moral obligation ranged from the rules of war, such as the treatment of prisoners and non-combatants, to the rights of man and the responsibility of states, especially the great powers, to put pressure on other states to treat their individual subjects more in accordance with what, in the nineteenth century, were called standards of civilization. By this expression and its successors, Western governments and publics have meant standards which they regard as universal but are in fact formulated in communities that, as Heeren put it, "resemble each other in their manners, religion and degree of social improvement."[3]

Even at that early state-centred stage of our investigations, it was clear to us that insofar as standards of civilization referred to the way governments treated their own subjects, the significant unit of moral obligation was not the state but the individual human being. We noted the obvious contradiction between action or inducement across state borders on behalf of the subjects or citizens of an inadequately "civilized" state, and the equally strongly held principle that the internal affairs of an independent state were no business of other states.[4]

Wight associated the moral obligations of governments with a "Kantian" vision of a world society. The obligation of states towards individuals was an aspect of international politics, alongside the impersonal pressures inherent in any system of states (symbolized by Hobbes) and the rules and codes of conduct of an international society (symbolized by Grotius). The diagram on page 9 of Buzan's *From International to World Society?*[5] illustrates Wight's perception, which can now be seen as the beginning of a rich vein of international theory.

I have included, as Chapter 6 of this volume, a paper on Justice Between States written in 1976 because it, and especially the second half, shows my own early attempt to grapple with the role of states in a world society of individuals. This question has since become a major preoccupation of some international relations theorists.

No member of the Committee did more to crystallize its thinking than Hedley Bull. His decisive contribution was to spell out the concept of a society of genuinely independent states: that is, an "anarchical" society free of any overarching authority able to enforce decisions. How I saw my discussions with Bull on these subjects is set out in Chapter 4, entitled Hedley Bull, States Systems and International Societies, and Chapter 5, The Anarchical Society in the History of International Relations: Discussions with Hedley Bull.

In the discussions about Bull's anarchical society, a major question for the historically minded members of the Committee was the uniqueness of the present arrangements. Were both the theory and the practice of the "European system" *sui generis*, as Butterfield suggested, something new and different in kind from what had gone before? Or was it simply the most developed example of the various rules and practices of past and present systems?[6]

A second issue was the cultural roots of moral obligation. How far did the rules and conventions of the European *grande république* differ in kind from the looser arrangements with the alien Ottomans; or for instance the society of classical Greek states differ from the arrangements with the Persian empire? We had identified as the essence of a society that its members consciously put in place elaborate rules and institutions to manage their involvement. But both the Ottoman and Persian wider systems did so too. However, I did not doubt that there were real differences, of kind as well as degree, between unicultural societies whose practice seemed largely determined by shared beliefs and customs, and wider arrangements that were mainly based on expediency. Butterfield put his finger on the importance of a common culture. His summary of the Committee's deliberations to the end of 1964 says that "The salient fact about the international systems so far studied is that basically they do not seem to have been produced by the process of bringing together units which have hitherto been quite separate. The effective force making for some sort of combination may be the elements of an antecedent common culture." Bull's view of an international society seemed to me more mechanical, with its values incidental rather than the root from which the society grew. He spoke of states which formed a society "recognising certain common interests and perhaps some common values."[7] Here, he was in accord with some proponents of a world society who doubt

4   Introduction: A voyage of exploration

the role of cultural differences. During our joint editing of *The Expansion of International Society*,[8] Bull and I were well aware of the cultural question, and perhaps moved some way towards an answer.

There is now an active debate in Europe about whether a shared cultural matrix is even more necessary if a closer union or confederacy is to hand over much more sovereignty to central authorities than is the case in our present world-wide international society. It points up the problem of how to bring in communities that do not share some or all of the cultural values of the "European social model." The question is not merely academic: it is particularly relevant to the extent and coherence of the European Union and, indeed in the cases of Turkey and Ukraine, to the meaning of the word Europe.

Once I retired from the Foreign Office in 1968, I was able to work more actively on my general comparative study of present and previous states systems. The British Committee had produced some valuable discussions and papers on past and present systems. When it decided to abandon the idea of a collective volume on the subject, I undertook to the Committee to compile a book describing and comparing the known systems, together with such general hypotheses about their functioning as the facts seemed to permit. I made it clear that my exploration of this aspect of the subject was to be my own. In a paper to the Committee, I said "It has always been understood that though my book grew out of the Committee's deliberations and would use them as something more than merely a point of departure, the book would set out my own ideas and I should not be limited by the Committee's discussions or confine myself to being a rapporteur."[9]

In 1970, I began, intermittently, the research and reflection needed. On 15 June 1972, I wrote to Herbert Butterfield: "I am trying to write down what I think about hegemony and anti-hegemonial coalitions, and the fact that if one state in a newtonian system increases its mass relative to the others by perfectly legitimate means, it still becomes an increasing potential threat to its neighbours. Of course, as a state does become stronger, it is bound to use its strength to have contested issues decided its way; and the anti-hegemonial coalition will find plenty of good reasons for resistance . . . I also find myself coming back to those factors which impede the smooth functioning of a newtonian balance of power—the non-vital interests of states and dynasties and communities, that militate against raison d'etat . . . So you see my book is getting away from our discussion in the Committee and moving on to hobby horses of my own, started by the themes in our original plan."[10]

In the 1980s, I taught a course of lectures on the subject at the University of Virginia. The task was not easy. Nobody can be an expert on all the systems of states about which we have a useful body of knowledge. Historians of present and past international relations have tended to focus on the policies of individual states rather than the workings of the system. I asked myself, and my students, how our present global system, with rules and institutions derived largely from Europe, came to constitute some 200 nominally sovereign states. The system is, I wrote, "puzzling if looked at in isolation"; and its practices are constantly changing. A comparison with past systems seemed to me the most effective way to see what is characteristic of states systems in general, and what is peculiar to our system in our time. My study of the subject finally crystallized as my book, *The Evolution of International Society*, which was published in 1992.

In their *International Systems in World History*,[11] published in 2000, Buzan and Little list three common faults of international theorists: eurocentrism, ahistoricism and anarchophilia. I have long felt the same concern. I think I can fairly claim that my book (which appeared some years earlier) avoids these faults; and also recognizes the role played in a system by dependent and "protected" states, which is often ignored by scholars. But my book deals only tangentially with the relation of states to individuals. That aspect of international politics, and the consequent erosion of the sovereign independence of states, took on increasing significance for me since it was first mooted in the British Committee. But even so, the state retains its centrality in international relations. It therefore seemed to me necessary to produce an adequate comparative analysis specifically of past and present systems of states across the wide spectrum of their diversity, as an aid to understanding where our present system came from and where it may be headed.

As *The Evolution of International Society* took shape in my mind, it also seemed to me that the study of past systems and societies of states sheds new light on the historical story as it emerges from the unrecorded past. I was encouraged to find that in their *International Systems in World History*, Buzan and Little focused on the insight which international relations theory can bring to our understanding of world history.

Chapter 7 of *Hegemony & History*, The Prospects for a More Integrated International Society, and Chapter 8, "The Practice Outruns the Theory", mark further stages in my voyage of exploration. They illustrate my evolving perception of a specific aspect of international relations theory, the ubiquity of some degree of hegemony in the anarchical half of the spectrum, illustrated by the current trend towards a more integrated, that is a more hegemonially managed, international order.

My Foreign Office assignments in the late 1950s and early 1960s—Head of the then continent-wide African Department of the Foreign Office, followed by Minister with a roving commission on decolonization in West Africa, and then Ambassador to Cuba—had led me to think hard about the place in our international society of small and weak states incapable of real independence in the sense of being able to manage modern statehood without considerable outside aid. I began to see the new international order that emerged from wholesale decolonization not only in Westphalian terms. It could also be seen as a core of economically and politically developed states, surrounded by an ever more numerous periphery of weak and inexperienced states faced often with the alternatives of firm government or chaos.

6 *Introduction: A voyage of exploration*

The decolonization that began in South and South East Asia and continued through to the collapse of the Soviet Union was an immense swing of the pendulum towards the anarchical or multi-independence end of the spectrum. The governments of the newly emancipated states had learnt to think in Westphalian terms. They wanted to become members of international society; but with few exceptions they wanted its legitimacy to be as loose and as little integrated as possible. Two major trends militated against this aim and undermined it. The first was the steady tightening of the network of economic pressures that continues to pull the system relentlessly towards integration and globalization. The second was the growing pressure of public and media opinion in Western and donor countries in favour of inducements and intervention to promote Western standards of civilization in recipient states in return for aid. A request from India for a contribution to a Festschrift in honour of Professor A.P. Rana, who has done much to clarify my mind on these issues, provided an opportunity to look at them, and at the trend towards a more hegemonial society, from a recipient point of view. My essay, entitled "The Prospects for a More Integrated International Society", is reproduced as Chapter 7 of this book.

By the 1980s, those in search of an adequate international theory were concentrating less exclusively on the relations between states and governments, and paying more attention to individuals. At the same time, Western political leaders were becoming more concerned with human rights, poverty, disease and other sufferings of individuals in less developed countries. This broadening of scope throws new light on the motivations and policies of states in today's world, and also on our understanding of the past.

One vivid example which has been in my mind in pursuing this line of thought is the role of individuals in the European wars of religion that followed the Reformation. Catholics felt a loyalty to the champions of their faith like the Habsburgs and Guises, and Protestants were drawn to the anti-hegemonial coalition. In some areas, only a minority were animated by loyalty to their prince and his state. There was massive migration of dissidents from both sides, to escape persecution and live under a more acceptable government. The movement of individuals "voting with their feet" enabled even the humblest individuals to have a greater say in how they were governed. At the same time, it gave to even petty rulers loyal subjects in place of dissidents, and so increased their power and independence. As Butterfield put it, there was a wind blowing in favour of kings. I would say that massive migration was one of the forces that pushed the European *grande république* towards the anarchic end of the spectrum and towards the Westphalian settlement.

The result of my exploration of the donor—recipient pattern is shown in Chapter 9, The Future of the Westphalian Anti-hegemonial International System, and Chapter 10, International Relations and the Practice of Hegemony. Finally in the 1990s, with encouragement by George Kennan, my views crystallized into another book, *The Limits of Independence*.[12] That book discusses: first the inadequacy of the sovereign state as the basic institution of government in Europe; then the consequences for the states system of decolonization and the creation of a host of incompetent nation states. It also discusses the relation of the new donor-recipient pattern to the practice of hegemony, and the growth in the developed donor core of a sense of responsibility for the condition of individuals in other states. Chapter 4 of *The Limits of Independence* reproduces the substantive part of a paper on some of these problems that I wrote for the Committee on my return from Havana in 1966.

Hegemony in the context of our current international society's Westphalian legitimacy is also discussed in Chapter 8, "The Practice Outruns the Theory", written in the late 1980s. At that time, as in 1960 when I began my voyage of exploration, many scholars and practitioners considered an anarchical society to be the desirable norm, and the West's well-established hegemonic practice to be at best a benign aberration rather than the virtually inevitable result of the pressure of world forces. The area of Soviet domination seemed even less legitimate to all those who did not accept the Soviet doctrine of Kremlin dominion of nominally independent states through subservient communist parties. Indeed the Soviets thought it prudent to pay lip service to the Westphalian legitimacy of multiple independences in Eastern Europe and elsewhere. How far removed is present practice from the theoretical ideal of a society of equal and independent states that we now call Westphalian; and how much legitimacy does the Westphalian ideal still retain? My present views on these questions are in the last chapter.

The members of the early British Committee also wanted to include economics in the scope of our investigations. The economic factor made up a large part of both the impersonal pressures of systems and the rules of a society. We were unable to find a suitable academic economist. I proposed Sir William Armstrong, then head of the permanent staff of the Treasury, whose familiarity with international economic negotiations enabled him to see what we were looking for; but he and ourselves realized that he could not provide an adequate answer. We realized that our failure in this area left a conspicuous gap. But we did not—at least I did not—yet perceive the role of economic activity in international systems as we see it today. My growing awareness of this role is reflected in the more recent papers in this book, especially Chapter 10.

The most powerful category in the sector is commercial corporations wanting to make money. The operations of private business stimulate and organize the production of goods and services for export across the administrative borders of states, and so create purchasing power to import in return. Some private economic enterprises—international oil companies and certain banks, for instance—make a profit by bringing supply to meet demand worldwide without commitment or allegiance to any particular state.

I found a useful textbook example of the role which a community's economic reach can play in a system, to be Venice at the height of its power.

8 *Introduction: A voyage of exploration*

Historical atlases show Venice with a small heartland at the head of the Adriatic and a chain of bases along the Balkans coast and into the eastern Mediterranean: but no more. The bases were a means, necessary stepping stones to Venetian commerce with the Levant, the Ottoman Empire that was a major part of the Euro-Mediterranean strategic and economic system. Once the goods bought in the Levant reached Venice they had to be safely transported over the Alps to northern Europe, and European goods brought safely back to be sold in the East; thus involving the business rulers of the "Most Serene Republic" in the entangling politics of the routes and markets of Europe. A realistic map would have to show thick tentacles of Venetian trade reaching out both ways, and in the east beyond the Ottoman domains to India and the spice islands. And of course a similar pattern would be needed for other maritime trading city states. The general question of economic radiation beyond administrative boundaries is well discussed in Part III of Buzan and Little's *International Systems in World History*.

In the early 1970s, as a result of thinking about the state–individual relationship I began to attach more importance to the ability of non-governmental organizations to influence relations between states, which has been less systematically examined than inter-state relations. In developed open societies the non-governmental area of relations is greater than the area of direct relations between their governments. The focus of many contributors to the English School was shifting to these non-state aspects; and in particular to the economic reach of a community beyond the administrative borders of its government. I thought we should not limit the private sector to "non-profit" organizations which champion moral causes. They seemed to me to be in the same general relation to international politics as religious organizations committed to spreading their sectarian beliefs, and economic enterprises. But I recognize that semantically the consensus uses non-governmental organizations (NGOs) to refer only to disinterested organizations advocating moral responsibility.

By the turn of the century, a considerable area of international relations theory had been explored, both in America and in Europe. Our perceptions of reality, and the reality itself, were changing. It was also time for me, as I approached the age of ninety, to leave further exploration to younger scholars. I looked for a chance to indicate to the next generation some of the areas which I thought needed further study. An opportunity occurred at the University of Copenhagen, under the auspices of Professor Ole Wæver who has been a major contributor to the English School. My remarks are reproduced in Chapter 11, entitled The Changing International System.

The last two chapters of the book are concerned specifically with hegemony. Chapter 12, entitled 1878: A Case Study in Collective Hegemony, is intended as an historical illustration of how a particular case of this under-studied form of hegemony functioned in practice. In the concluding chapter, Hegemony & History, I set out my view of the general nature of hegemony, and the light which the historical evidence throws on its operation. This final chapter brings down to the present my exploration of an area of international political theory which began when I realized that although the European system was nominally an anarchical society of independent states, it was in fact a succession of hegemonies.

2 The British Committee on the Theory of International Politics

I was greatly encouraged by the present proposal to relaunch the concentrated dialogue of the British Committee for the Theory of International Politics, and by the positive response of the many leading scholars listed in Barry Buzan's article "The English School: an Underexploited Resource in International Relations."

The working methods of the original Committee are well summarized in Buzan's article, and those methods and the scope of its enquiries are described more fully in Tim Dunne's most useful history of the English School of International Relations, *Inventing International Society*.[1] There is thus no need to look back over them here.

The Committee's interdisciplinary composition, with practitioners alongside academics, exploratory discussions groping after theory, and the readiness of its members to be influenced by each other, did help to produce significant results, and can as Buzan suggests be usefully adapted to further examination of international relations theory and the gap between it and the current practices of the system. The contribution of practitioners is less visible because they do not normally publish papers on international relations theory. In selecting future practitioners it will be well to remember that the role of conventional diplomacy—Foreign Ministries, embassies and so on—is declining with the development of technology and the transformation to an ever less Westphalian system. Future study groups will need to extend the range of practitioner experience beyond diplomacy to cover economic globalization and other effects of increasing interdependence.

When we come to the intellectual agenda of the study groups, it is clear that they will have to ask themselves new questions. Buzan's proposal lists six themes, which cover a very adequate range of subjects and academic disciplines, and enable future working groups to start from where the work of the Committee and subsequent English School scholars has reached.

From the first the Committee focused its attention on the structure and the practices of the European system, which Hedley Bull led us to understand as an anarchical society. We noted that in its world-wide expansion, its rules and institutions and its standards of civilization remained essentially European. Some of us were inclined to treat the existing society as unique, the only one worth studying, and also to view it as the implementation in practice of what came to be called the Westphalian theory of absolute and juridically equal independences. Butterfield and Bull were less interested in other systems, especially those whose members were unable to conduct an independent foreign policy.

Martin Wight and I were the unhappiest about this limitation. We felt that in our search for a theory we needed also to study systems where some or most of the political entities were in varying degrees dependent. He and I wanted especially to discuss hegemonies and suzerain systems, where partially dependent states retained nominal independence and a high degree of autonomy in practice. Wight used to argue that the European system was what we call Westphalian only for brief periods, and was mainly a succession of hegemonies. It seemed to me that once you took to looking at the structure and the practice of past hegemonial and imperial systems, the world-wide one of the nineteenth and twentieth centuries ceased to seem so unique and so anarchical, and appeared as one of a set of historical systems; and indeed one with pronounced hegemonial characteristics, quite a way along the spectrum of possible patterns. However the Committee did not get around to serious study of hegemonial and suzerain systems.

These ideas or hunches, and the groundwork laid by the Committee's discussions and papers on other systems, led me to begin the compilation of my *Evolution of International Society*.[2] I had much help and advice from Butterfield and Bull, who in our discussions both recognized that the comparison with past systems could throw light on the present one. The popular Zeitgeist of the decolonization age relegated hegemonies and empires to "the dustbin of history", and asserted that Westphalian independent statehood was the only politically acceptable formula. So it was good to find that nevertheless a number of younger scholars in Britain and elsewhere were producing serious comparative studies of past hegemonial and imperial systems.

Most significantly there is the work of Barry Buzan and Richard Little. Papers like "A Long Look Back" and "Reconceptualizing International Relations" effectively developed the wider perspective that Wight and I considered essential. Their monumental new book *International Systems in World History*[3] refashions the study of international relations: taking it back to its very beginnings in the indispensable contacts between hunter-gatherer bands, and spelling out a coherent and comprehensive theory for the whole set of recorded and deducible practices. Notably their splendid Chapter 17, "What World History Tells Us about International Theory", and their last summarizing chapter seem to me the fulfilment of what Wight and I had in mind as a necessary basis for further study. The whole book, and especially those chapters, will surely provide a milestone text for the proposed future discussions.

By now the battle against ahistorical and eurocentric limitations on international theory has largely been won. In Buzan and Little's vivid phrase, international relations studies are out of the Westphalian ghetto. But "anarchophilia" (to use their term) is still with us; especially the view that the only system relevant to the contemporary world is relations between independent states. The nominal constitution of the system, as reflected in the United Nations and international law, is indeed some two hundred separate and sovereign states. But in fact the practice of the system has moved far from the Westphalian assumptions.

Among the general questions which future working groups should address, we may note the following. Is the practice of the system best described as a collective hegemony of the most developed Western states? Or is it rather like a series of concentric circles, with a core group centred round the United States dealing with a periphery of failed and incompetent states and quasi-states as well as other more independent ones? How far is the collective hegemony, or the core, impelled by both prudence and moral obligation to aid and intervene in those states that cannot manage for themselves? Is this aid and intervention a net benefit to the periphery and the world as a whole, even though it is not positive enough to satisfy Western publics and not always carried out wisely or well? What lines of continuity, and what differences, can we see between present practice and earlier colonial and trusteeship regimes and attempts to impose Western standards on China and elsewhere? What changes will the development and diffusion of technology bring to relations between the wide range of political entities in the global system?

Certainly the most conspicuous aspect of hegemonial intervention, namely peacemaking and peacekeeping where practice has so obviously outrun Westphalian theory, needs more study. Non-intervention, once considered a cornerstone of international order, is now widely condemned as the failure of the core to meet its international responsibilities. But military intervention is occasional and localized, mainly concerned with warfare within peripheral states. Moreover, we can discern serious attempts to revise both international relations theory and the legitimacy of present practices in this area. Already in 1984 Dame Rosalyn Higgins, now the British representative at the International Court of Justice at The Hague, wrote that the task of international lawyers on intervention was "not to go on repeating the rhetoric of dead events which no longer accord with reality, but to try to assist the political leaders to identify what is the new (i.e. post-Westphalian) consensus."[4] We also see the great powers reshaping their armed forces away from conflict with each other and towards collective intervention in the periphery.

More significant, I think, and much less analysed by existing international relations theory, are two world-wide, sustained and growing fields of interaction: economic; and cultural, including standards of civilization. Above all, it seems to me that international relations theoretical analysis of the role of economic factors is still inadequate. One dramatic insight of Buzan and Little's book is the major role played by economic and cultural exchanges in knitting the world together. This has been so from the interaction between hunter-gatherer bands before states existed, through the trade between Rome, India and China to the economically motivated global expansion of the European system.

The more developed core societies need a healthy global economy. To maintain it they provide continuous world-wide coordinated help of various kinds to the periphery. Donor states do so both directly and through international agencies like the World Bank and the International Monetary Fund which they control. The core operates a huge and still somewhat experimental centrifuge to the periphery. It provides material goods, or money to buy them; technology, training and know-how; and markets in core economies for goods from the periphery. More than half the transfer of resources is purveyed or mediated by private enterprise; and therefore so long as the peripheral states retain enough effective autonomy to set the terms, it needs to offer benefits to both parties.

The mainly Western donors demand in return the observance of their standards of civilization—human rights, democracy, social justice and the environment. These standards are too difficult for many peripheral states where the practical alternatives are firm government or chaos. Even so, peripheral governments increasingly observe Western standards as the price of aid. Will these trends with their distributive overtones continue? Or can newer states expect to become weaned from their present dependence? How far is the influence of the great Asian powers—China, Japan, India—in the hegemonial concert likely to grow, making standards of civilization, and especially concepts of justice, less exclusively Western? These are issues of special concern to policy-oriented working groups.

Today's collective hegemony makes the world more integrated and safer, and less anarchic. How far does this process limit the freedom of action of all states, even the largest? How far is it eroding, and might it continue to erode, not only sovereignty but the basic premise of Westphalian theory, the state itself?

Western aid and hegemonial intervention have both ethical and profitable motives. Aid and globalization, and the hunger of the periphery for more equably distributed prosperity, provide a lever for the West to promote its cultural values. This lever, by which economic practice moves the Western cultural and ethical agenda, is perhaps the greatest dynamic of the contemporary international system. Can we say that this has been true since decolonization, though the picture was obscured by the strategic preoccupations of the Cold War? Even so, hegemonial authority and globalization still lack legitimacy. A future enquiry might well go beyond the limits of theory to examine how the present tentative structure of international society can be made both more effective and more legitimate. Incorporating this pervasive practice into a general international relations theory is surely a major task for the reconvened English School. I hope particular attention will be paid to the role of economics and culture in these wider senses.

3 Martin Wight and the Theory of International Relations*

One aspect of international relations which interested Martin Wight particularly was the functioning of what are called systems of states. That has also been an area of my especial interest since the late 1950s. It was the focus of the discussions of the British Committee on the Theory of International Politics. The Committee was organized in the late fifties to bring together people from different disciplines, practitioners as well as scholars. Herbert Butterfield and Martin were the founders and guiding spirits of the early years of the Committee, and I was one of the original members. It was a collective enterprise: members submitted papers which left as questions those points on which the author did not feel certain of the answers. Martin told me that the most stimulating and interesting work he did during the 1960s was writing papers for the Committee and taking part in its discussions.

The papers which Martin wrote for the Committee about the functioning of states systems were published after his death by Hedley Bull. Perhaps the most important is the general analysis which he called *De systematibus civitatum*, from the essay by Pufendorf in 1675 which defined the concept and gave it its name.[1] The paper followed several discussions by the Committee and a number of essays, notably Martin's "Why is there no International Theory?" and others by Herbert Butterfield, Desmond Williams and myself.[2] "My aim in the present paper", Martin began, "is to offer some notes towards clarifying the idea of a states system and to formulate some of the questions or propositions which a comparative study of states systems would examine ... the kind of issue which I believe we should discuss systematically."[3] The paper summed up the problems with Martin's unique combination of clarity, scholarship and thoroughness.

De systematibus greatly clarified our minds. It has also provided since then a focus for my own thinking on the subject of states systems, and in particular a point of departure for the book on that subject which I am now completing. I can best illustrate the continuity between Martin's work and

---

* This is an edited text of the 1989 Martin Wight Memorial Lecture given at The London School of Economics.

mine by quoting Herbert Butterfield's first Martin Wight Memorial Lecture. "When we decided to make a prolonged study of States Systems in various parts of the globe throughout the ages, [Martin] took a leading part in the discussions; and we hope that the stimulus of these will secure that Adam Watson will complete his own book on systems of states."[4] I therefore want to remind you of the questions which Martin formulated and the assumptions which underlay them; and to set out for you briefly some results of my subsequent work on the subject, indicating how I would now answer Martin's questions.

Types of states systems

First the *scope* of the subject. The European states system, leading to the present world-wide one, is not unique. There have been several others. We set out to compare the historical evidence, and see what the systems "in various parts of the globe throughout the ages" have in common and how they differ. *De systematibus* listed three agreed examples of states systems: the Western, the Greco-Roman, and the Chinese of the Warring States; and mentioned the Indian and other systems. The opinion of some scholars, that no other system is comparable to the European one, seemed to us to be based on too narrow and parochial a concept of what constitutes a state, and of what constitutes a system.

By states we conventionally mean sovereign states—independent political authorities which recognize no superior. For states to form a system each must, in Martin's formulation of the accepted view, "recognise the same claim to independence by all the others." The sovereigns of the European system did this, and so did the Greek city states and Hellenistic kingdoms. But Martin did not want us to stop there. He cited the ancient Chinese system, the Roman system, and even the British Raj in India as examples of groups of states in permanent relations with one another, "but one among them asserts unique claims which the others formally or tacitly accept." Notice the phrase "or tacitly." Since the claim in such systems was to suzerainty, Martin suggested that "we might distinguish them from international states systems by calling them suzerain states systems."[5] He wanted us to look at both.

Level of cultural unity

Let us now turn to two more fundamental sets of questions. The first concerns *cultural unity*. "We must assume", says *De systematibus*, "that a states system will not come into being without a degree of cultural unity among its members."[6] If we accept the assumption, do the code of conduct and the institutions of each system reflect the distinct values and religion of its common culture, or are the agreed rules essentially regulatory, conditioned by the same empirical pressures in all systems?

Now if by a system we mean any group of states or communities so involved with one another that each is obliged to take continuous account of what the others do, and therefore they are in regular communication and perhaps conflict with each other, then obviously the members of a system will sometimes belong to different cultures. The relations between the Egyptian and Hittite empires and their clients at the time of the Tell el Amarna tablets are an example. The diplomatic dialogue was conducted in cuneiform Aramaic, and indeed the negotiations seem to have developed in an Aramaic, that is a Syrian, context; yet neither Egypt nor the Hittites belonged to the Aramaic culture. On the other hand where we have what Hedley Bull calls an *international society*, with consciously formulated rules and institutions reinforced by shared assumptions and values, the historical evidence fully supports Martin's assumption.[7] Indeed I know of no international society that did not originate inside a single dominant culture.

Hedley Bull formulated his seminal distinction, between the impersonal pressures of a system and the consciously formulated rules of a society, after and as a result of *De systematibus*. Martin's use of the term "states system" reflects an older and wider usage. His assumption about cultural unity is shared by previous scholars, from Pufendorf to Spengler and Toynbee. Heeren's classic formula in the preface to the *Geschichte des Europaeischen Staatensystems*, quoted by Martin, defines a states system as "the union of several contiguous states, resembling each other in their manners, religion and degree of social improvement, and cemented together by a reciprocity of interests." That definition of a states system is close to Bull's definition of a society, specifically limited to a single culture. Voltaire in the striking second chapter of his *Siècle de Louis XIV* called Europe, give or take Russia, "une grande république"—one great commonwealth—divided into several states; and he described its shared cultural practices, which excluded the Ottoman Turks.

While families of states (to use a biological metaphor) like Hellas and the European *grande république* developed complex inter-state societies within the framework of a culture, some more purely regulatory machinery, on what we might call Tell el Amarna lines, is also necessary for the operation, the orderliness, of a system that extends beyond a single culture. The most striking example is the arrangements between the *grande république* and the Ottoman Empire. The Ottoman Empire controlled about a quarter of Europe in the seventeenth and eighteenth centuries; and it was militarily so powerful, and economically so interesting, that every Christian state had to take it into account. Its informal cooperation with France and the Protestant states broke the Habsburg hegemony and made Europe safe for protestantism, and its later policies contributed to the defeats of Louis XIV and Napoleon. Yet it was not part of the European international society, and disdained that society's rules, institutions and peace settlements. Instead the Ottomans developed a separate regulatory code of conduct with the European states, known as *capitulations*; which were largely prescribed by the Ottomans in the heyday of their power, but later modified by the Europeans in their own favour when they became stronger.

When the nineteenth-century European expansion involved the whole world in a single system of economic and strategic pressures, we find the Europeans using the capitulations with the Ottomans as a model for dealing with countries with different cultures like China and Morocco, more than the arrangements of their own much more closely knit *grande république*. The difference between the culturally conditioned rules and institutions of the European society and the capitulatory arrangements with the Ottomans seems to me to deserve more careful study, because it provides a valuable clue to our understanding of states systems and their relation to a cultural framework.

However, the position is more complicated than that. Once an international society in Hedley Bull's sense has come into being within the matrix of a culture, its regulatory rules and institutions, and to a much less extent its values, can and do spread beyond its original members. The transformation of the European system into our present global one offers many examples of states from other cultures graduating, so to speak, from capitulations to accepting the rules and being admitted to full membership of the international society that originated in Europe. But it was the states of the enlarged *grande république*, which by now included Russia and the United States, that decided who should be admitted to membership of their club.

I therefore now think it more accurate to say that the formal rules and institutions of a *society* of states, and even more its codes of conduct and its unspoken assumptions, are formed within the matrix of a single culture; but states belonging to other cultures that find themselves involved in the pressures of the same system can become members of the society or be associated with it, provided they accept its rules and assumptions, perhaps with marginal modifications.

Degrees of hegemony

The second set of questions raised by Martin concerns *hegemony*. This issue particularly interested him and me. We both wanted to look beyond systems composed of equally independent states, to hierarchy and hegemony, because that is how most systems actually function much of the time. "Is there always a hierarchy between states in a system?" Martin asked in *De systematibus*. Are there always great powers with recognized special rights and responsibilities? He suspected that hegemony by the power or powers at the top of the hierarchy was usual and perhaps ubiquitous. He called the European system "a succession of hegemonies, in which one great power after another tries to transform the states system, or even to abolish it." One answer to hegemony is a balance of power; and he asked "Does the balance of power system arise only in response to the threat of hegemony?"[8]

Furthermore, Martin said, once you examine the workings of hegemony, and the historical record, you come up against the prospect that sooner or later the strongest power in the system will tighten its grip beyond hegemony, and establish an empire. That is what happened in the China of the Warring States; it is what happened in the Greco-Roman system, and nearly happened under Alexander, it is what happened in ancient India when the system of independent kingdoms described in the Arthashastra was unified into the Maurya Empire. Martin feared that the mechanism of the balance of power, and substitutes for it like the League of Nations, were bound to fail sooner or later. In *De systematibus* he stated that "most state systems have ended in a universal empire, which has swallowed all the states of the system", and asked whether we knew of any states system which did not. He saw this as an unconventional and pessimistic question. He intended to write a paper for us describing how the Hellenistic system of independent states was gradually transformed into a Roman suzerain system and finally into an empire. It has been a real disappointment to me that he did not write that paper.

If hegemony is so prevalent in systems of independent states, how do they differ from suzerain systems? In suzerain systems, Martin said, one power makes a unique claim, to determine the rules and institutions of the system —or as we would now say, the society. But that is also the claim of the hegemonial power of the day in the European society and in city state Greece. The difference which we had in mind was that in suzerain societies the suzerain is the *legitimate* source of hegemonial authority: that is to say, the other states formally or tacitly accept the *principle* that there should be a suzerainty, though they sometimes reject the claim of a particular ruler to exercise it. By contrast, the other states in the European and Greek societies reject the principle, though they may acquiesce in a hegemony in practice.

In the 1960s we attached great importance to this distinction. Herbert Butterfield said that once the states in a system ceased to assert their independence and accepted a hegemony, the system ceased to be interesting; and Hedley Bull's classic work, *The Anarchical Society*, which grew out of papers written for the Committee, stops at the same dividing line. The distinction still seems fundamental to many scholars today. Martin called our attitude a matter of judgement. "Why", he asked, "are we inclined to judge a system of [independent] states as a more desirable way of arranging the affairs of a great number of men than the alternatives?"[9]

There were perhaps three reasons for the way we thought at that time. First, it was the conventional wisdom, from which we were only beginning to free ourselves. Second, the European system since Westphalia—that is, during most of its existence—has theoretically been a society of independent states which all recognize each other as such. The Committee accepted the theory. We thought of the hegemonial practice as a series of violations of the legitimate society, which the anti-hegemonial coalitions were each time fortunately able to defeat. Third, in the world as a whole the 1960s were the culmination of the historic drive for the independence of dependent states, the wholesale decolonization of the Western overseas empires, what Professor Kedourie has called the Chatham House version of history. Multiple independences seemed to us legitimate and desirable, and also assured in the short term. Martin's pessimistic question about all systems ending in empires referred to developments beyond the horizon.

I would like to offer to you here a comment on what I have just said, by Professor Inis Claude, one of the most distinguished American thinkers on the subject. "This seems to me", he writes, "a quintissentially European view. I was nurtured on the Wilsonian critique of the European states system and the accompanying conviction that a multistate system is incorrigibly productive of catastrophic disorder. In my setting and my generation, the conventional wisdom had it that 'One World' was essential, and that a system of multiple sovereignties was a recipe for disaster."[10] In other words, we really do need some supranational machinery for maintaining order, for managing international society, more than just law and balance between independent states.

A spectrum of systems

The discussion so far has assumed that there is an important dividing line between independence and hegemony. I have since become increasingly doubtful about sharp distinctions between systems of independent states, suzerain systems and empires. I now prefer to define the wider subject by saying that, when a number of diverse communities of people, or political entities, are sufficiently involved with one another for us to describe them as forming a *system* of some kind (whether independent, suzerain or whatever), the organization of the system will fall somewhere along a notional *spectrum* between absolute independence and absolute empire. The two marginal positions are theoretical absolutes, that do not occur in practice.

It is convenient for purposes of comparison to divide the spectrum into four broad categories of relationship: independence, hegemony, dominion and empire. In practice these categories are not watertight, with an abrupt transition from one to another. The range of states systems is rather a continuum, like wavelengths of light in a rainbow, which we find it convenient to divide into different colours. As the wavelengths of green light get longer, the light gets bluer; and so, as the external freedom of action of communities in a system decreases, the more hegemonial the system becomes. But there is no clear dividing line. We must be careful not to give more importance to the distinctions we make between colours or categories than they really have. But we should also be careful not to say that the complexity of history makes the enterprise of drawing distinctions a useless one.

Independent states in a system indicates political entities that retain the ultimate ability to take external decisions as well as domestic ones. But we all agree that in practice freedom in external decisions is limited by two factors. First, the constraints which involvement in any system imposes;

and second, the voluntary commitments that states assume in order to manage their external relations more effectively. The greater the constraints and commitments, the tighter the system will be, and the further along the spectrum away from absolute independences.

The more closely so-called sovereign states are involved with each other, the less they feel able to operate alone. The impersonal net of strategic and economic pressures that hold them together in a system induces them to make alliances, trade treaties and so on. Alliances and other agreements bring a form of *order* to what would be an inchoate system by coordinating, and thus modifying, the behaviour of their members. That is an aspect of what the European system called *raison d'état*. (Herbert Butterfield's first Martin Wight Memorial Lecture, entitled "Raison d'État", was addressed to the development of these ideas.) Order is further promoted by general agreements and rules that restrain and benefit all members of the system, and make it into a society. That is an aspect of *raison de système*, the belief that it pays to make the system work. Insofar as such agreements are truly voluntary, and are not laid down by a victor power or group of powers, they fall within the multiple independences area of the spectrum.

But the freedom of action of independent states is not only limited by the pressures of interdependence and by voluntary choice. Usually it is also limited, more effectively, by *hegemony*. By a hegemony I mean that some power or authority in a system is able to "lay down the law" about the operation of the system, that is to determine to some extent the relations *between* member states, while leaving them domestically independent. Some scholars like to reserve the term hegemony for the exercise of this authority by a single power, but it is obvious that the authority can be exercised either by an individual power, or as is often the case by a small group. An example of dual hegemony is the Athenian–Spartan diarchy after the Persian wars. Kimon told his fellow Athenians that they and the Spartans were like a pair of oxen yoked together for the task, and warned them not to kick against their yokefellow. The five great European powers after 1815 exercised a diffused hegemony, which I will discuss in a moment. Indeed the rules and institutions of the European international society were far from purely voluntary: they were to a large extent *imposed* by the principal victors at the great peace settlements like Westphalia, Vienna and Versailles, and were to that extent hegemonial. I therefore prefer the wider use of the term hegemony, rather than ugly words like para-hegemonial. Moreover, like Martin I want to use the term hegemony in an objective rather than a pejorative sense. A hegemony is not a dictatorial *fiat*. The hegemonies which I have looked at, whether exercised by an individual power or a small group, involve continual dialogue between the hegemonial authority and the other states, and a sense on both sides of the balance of expediency.

Further along the spectrum *dominion* covers situations where an imperial authority to some extent determines government of other communities, but they nevertheless retain their identity and some control over their own affairs. Examples are Soviet relations with Eastern Europe before Gorbachev, the relation of the Emperor Augustus to Herod's kingdom, or the relation of the British Raj to the Indian princes. Here the part played by the ability to coerce becomes more obvious.

Finally *empire* means direct administration of different communities from an imperial centre. It is no more absolute in practice than independence: the freedom of action of imperial governments is limited by the constraints which any involvement with other communities imposes.

No known system remains fixed at one point in the spectrum. Systems tighten and loosen, and the relation of the various communities to each other shifts constantly to and fro along the spectrum over time. There is also a variation in space. Political entities—that is, communities held together by a common government—involved in a system do not all stand in the same relationship to each other, or to an imperial power. When looked at closely every relationship between two communities has in practice a special nature of its own. In addition the political entities which compose systems are far from being either all alike, or constants in themselves. The members of the European society, for instance, ranged from the nebulous presidential authority of the emperor and the many communities under the very real sovereignty or Hausmacht of the Habsburgs in Vienna, to states like Parma and Schaumburg-Lippe that were no more than the estates of petty princes. We must use terms like state and community also in as neutral a sense as possible.

We could represent our spectrum as vertical, with a gravitational pull from multiple independences at the top down through hegemony to dominion and empire. Martin might have seen it that way. I find that a more useful metaphor for understanding systems is the pendulum. Imagine the spectrum laid out in the form of an arc, with its midpoint at the bottom of the pendulum's swing, somewhere between hegemony and dominion. Was there in former systems, is there now, not merely oscillation to and fro, but a noticeable pendulum effect, in the sense of a gravitational pull on systems away from *both* the theoretical extremes and towards some central area of the spectrum, even though the momentum of change and other factors may carry the pendulum past that area? I am now (after twenty years of looking at the evidence) inclined to think that there is a pendulum effect, though the pattern varies from one system to another. We need to compare the pressures towards greater autonomy that make empires and dominions loosen and break up, with the corresponding tendencies towards hegemony in systems of independent states (which is what interested Martin). In the practical operation of states systems, as opposed to their formal legitimacy— de facto rather than de iure—the midpoint tends to be a varying degree of autonomy or domestic independence, ordered by a degree of external hegemony or authority, individual or joint.

The image of the pendulum is a way of illustrating the tension between the desire for order and the desire for independence. The desire for a balanced system, that is neither too tight nor too loose, causes the gravitational pull on the pendulum.

The emergence of rules

Why do political entities locked in a system obey rules? Coercion or the threat of coercion is a quite insufficient explanation. An important factor in the functioning of a states system is the degree to which its arrangements are accepted as legitimate. By *legitimacy* in this context I mean the acceptance of authority, the right of a rule or a ruler to be obeyed, as distinguished from the ability to coerce. Authority is determined not by those who wield it but by the attitudes of those who obey it. The historical evidence is that all systems, and especially international societies of states, operate largely on the basis of what their members consider legitimate authority, as opposed to compulsion or the threat of it, and that all member states or communities usually, and most of them all the time, abide by the rules. Legitimacy facilitates the exercise of authority in a system, and makes it more acceptable. It is not the motive force of the system, but it is perhaps the lubricating oil.

What are these rules, that enjoy the authority of legitimacy? Unlike the constitutions promulgated for the domestic government of some states, in international societies the practice occurs first. And the practice always has some element of hegemony in it. The practice is then codified into rules, and ad hoc arrangements are institutionalized. Time and custom legitimize practice. And so, in a different way, do the declarations of peace settlements. Inevitably the practices which were innovative and expedient at one phase of the system become rigid when they are codified and institutionalized. The legitimacy of the day oils and facilitates the functioning of the system within its accepted rules; but it holds back changes in the rules. Practice is fluid, and runs beyond the legitimacy. It tries out new expedients, some of which are discarded while others become legitimized and institutionalized in their turn. Grotius, the lawyer and professional diplomat, set out to codify and to make acceptable the untidy practice of his time, and found the practice changing as he formulated it. Professor Rosalyn Higgins is entirely in accord with my understanding of the working of international societies when she recently wrote: "The task of the international lawyer over the next few years is surely not to go on repeating the rhetoric of dead events which no longer accord with reality, but to try to assist the political leaders to identify what is the new consensus about acceptable and unacceptable" actions.[11]

The evolving European system

With these ideas in mind let us look again at the European society of states. Martin called it a succession of hegemonies. That is so, in the sense that the propensity to hegemony, the tendency to move away from the extreme of multiple independences, was always present: not as an aberration but as an *integral feature of the system*. First there were the Habsburgs, based on Spain and the Empire. They operated strictly within the legitimacy of the time as they understood it, and in particular the accepted rules of inheritance, which put their family in a hegemonial position. The anti-hegemonial coalition that destroyed the Habsburg hegemony operated on the basis of the de facto independence of its members; and the aims and practices of the victorious coalition became the public law of Europe. But the victors did not want an anarchic free-for-all: they wanted to replace the Habsburg hegemonial order by an anti-hegemonial order which operated by means of international law and a diplomatic dialogue. This was an imaginative and seminal concept, the basis of today's international legitimacy. But the new legitimacy of a commonwealth of sovereign states established at Westphalia leaned considerably further towards multiple independences than was warranted either by the distribution of power in Europe or by the innate propensity to hegemony and order in the system. Into this gap between the legitimacy and the reality stepped the hegemony of Louis XIV, himself half a Habsburg, married to a Habsburg wife and sovereign of the most powerful state in the system. Louis XIV managed his hegemony within the framework of the new Westphalian legitimacy, though not its spirit. He did this by a network of client allies which he subsidized, as the Persians did during the King's Peace in ancient Greece; by an unprecedented continuous diplomatic dialogue of threat and inducement; and by that ultimate argument, the actual use of force.

Between Louis and Napoleon, from the Utrecht settlement of 1714 to the French Revolution of 1789, the European sovereigns' club translated into practice the anti-hegemonial concepts of Utrecht and Westphalia. During those exceptional seventy-five years there was no hegemony in Europe, but an effective balance of power consciously operated by statesmen. Martin's question in *De systematibus* about the balance of power in other states systems led Herbert Butterfield to write his masterly paper on the balance of power, which shows that though a de facto equilibrium existed from time to time in other systems, the conscious aim of a general balance was present in the minds of statesmen for the first time in the European society of states. And we should note that the weights in the balance extended beyond the European sovereigns' club to include the Ottoman Empire.

Napoleon's imperial authority took the European society of states further away than ever before from the anti-hegemonial balance of power towards the empire end of our spectrum; and it altered men's ideas about managing that society. It is true that his defeat restored anti-hegemonial legitimacy. The Treaty of Vienna confirmed that all states in the *grande république* were to be regarded as juridically equal. But the statesmen who congregated at Vienna understood, more clearly than they are sometimes given credit for, the advantages of domestic and international order which Napoleon's empire, in spite of incessant external war, had brought to the great areas of Europe which he controlled. They thought it undesirable as well as impracticable to revert to the eighteenth-century practice.

Hitherto the most powerful state in the system and its allies had been opposed by a coalition led by the second most powerful state. Now the five most powerful European sovereigns (including a restored France) agreed that some authority was needed to maintain and modify the Vienna settlement. The five great powers did not trust each other to exercise a unilateral authority. But instead of opposing each other, as had hitherto been the anti-hegemonial practice, they formed a single partnership, sustained by concerted diplomacy, in order to arrogate to themselves the duties and privileges of operating a joint authority. That was what I think Martin had in mind when in *De systematibus* he asked the Committee to examine the institutionalizing of the special role of great powers after 1815. Where the five powers agreed to act together, checking and balancing each other, or at least acquiesced in action after consultation, they could collectively exercise a *diffused hegemony* which none would agree to another exercising alone. Acquiescence was a felicitous device of the shared hegemony. It enabled a great power to judiciously abstain from certain decisions and their enforcement, and so to maintain intact both its principles and its partnership in the concert. Harmony between them, when it was achieved, orchestrated the Concert of Europe. In a sense the Concert was a synthesis between two opposing ways of organizing Europe: it combined the hegemonic laying down of the law with the balance of power.

The great powers soon found that their interests and—more difficult—their principles diverged. They began to kick against their yokefellows. But they shared an interest in the successful operation of the new concert. The other member states of the European society resented their exclusion from the hegemony of the great powers, but they tacitly accepted it. The Concert acquired a certain legitimacy, which remained in existence even when the practice gradually weakened. This most diffuse of Martin's succession of hegemonies was the climax of European constructive achievement in the managing of a states system.

I need not elaborate the relevance of hegemony to the very different world of today. The five permanent members of the Security Council are an inadequate survival of the formal legitimacy of five great powers. In practice the global system from the end of the World War Two until today separated out into two main opposed hegemonial systems. But it seems to me that after our half of the system moved to extremes of decolonization and theoretical multiple independences in the 1960s, the pendulum is now swinging back towards more hegemonial forms of order. This is particularly visible in the economic field. A majority of the member states of our international society are politically autonomous but economically dependent, in the sense that they cannot and do not want to manage without considerable outside aid. We are witnessing the experiment of managing the economic affairs of the non-communist world by the collective hegemony of the Group of Seven, which includes all the great powers of our economic system. Of course the composition of the group may change, particularly if the four European members become more closely integrated. This economic hegemony is legitimated by operating through established collective machinery like the World Bank and the International Monetary Fund, as well as through client alliances like the Lomé conventions which are more reminiscent of Louis XIV's practices.

A political and strategic order would have to be world-wide. One way of managing it would be to extend the Concert by bringing in the Soviet Union and China. A global concert on these lines, using United Nations machinery to make its decisions more acceptable, is now politically conceivable. Some would say that in places like Angola and Indochina it is already in operation. Alternatively, I suppose the political hegemony of our global system might take the form of a diarchy of the two superpowers, maintaining an order agreed between them; which would be similar to the Athenian–Spartan diarchy after the Persian wars. Perhaps the Americans and the Russians are no longer strong enough, relative to the rest of us, to operate an effective diarchy; but where they agree, their combined weight is likely to prevail. In any case the question is not whether there will be some degree of hegemonial direction in our international affairs, but how much. In order to mitigate resentment, the practical arrangements for forms of joint hegemonial order are likely to be cloaked in the rhetoric of individual independence for every state, and are likely to use established omnilateral machinery where possible to implement hegemonial programmes. For, as I said, legitimacy is the lubricating oil of the society.

The way forward

I have said enough to show that Martin's questions about the nature of states systems brought a fresh wind of original and penetrating thought to the subject. By putting these questions to our committee, which included some of the most inquisitive minds in the field, and by helping to work out some answers, he carried the subject a significant stage forward. He was convinced, and confirmed my suspicion, that in order to achieve anything worthwhile, we must free ourselves both from the conventional historiography which imposed blinkers on our angle of vision, and did not ask the right questions; and also from the fashionable ideology of the day. As he put it, "the intellectual and moral poverty of international theory are due first to the intellectual prejudice imposed by the sovereign state, and secondly to the belief in progress." The search for detachment made him value the comparison with other states systems. Comparative analysis might help us to work out a general international theory, valid not only for the European but for all systems.

Of all Martin's questions, perhaps the most seminal for me were the ones which took us beyond systems made up only of independent states, to include hegemonial and suzerain systems. This enlargement of the horizon brought him to the realization that the European system too was not a system of free states operating in a balance that could put down periodic bids for hegemony but, in his illuminating phrase, a succession of hegemonies. We all felt the impact of this insight. Some years after Martin's death I showed Hedley Bull a draft of my work on states systems, and his comment was that what scholars would seize on as the outstanding feature of the work was the central role of hegemony in all systems. When I pointed out that the idea was originally Martin's, he said that seeds planted by Martin had developed also in his case into the Anarchical Society. I want in this lecture to place my debt to Martin on record. And also to record the hope that some of the younger scholars here will look again at *De systematibus* and "Why is there no International Theory?", and also at the work which Hedley Bull and I among many others have done since in this field. I hope they will take a stage further the search for answers to our questions, and perhaps work out a general theory covering the range of relations between political entities.

4 Hedley Bull, states systems and international societies

Hedley Bull's contribution to the theory of international relations is considerable; and nowhere more acute than in the distinction which he made between the concept of a system of states and that of an international society. His definitive formulation is set out in Chapter 1 of *The Anarchical Society*. "Where states are in regular contact with one another, and where in addition there is interaction between them sufficient to make the behaviour of each a necessary element in the calculations of the other, then we may speak of their forming a system."[1] "A society of states (or international society) exists when a group of states, conscious of certain common interests and common values, form a society in the sense that they conceive themselves to be bound by a common set of rules in their relations with one another, and share in the working of common institutions."[2]

The formula is clear and practical. He evolved it gradually, in order to distinguish between what he saw, both in the contemporary world and in the past, as groups of independent states held together by a web of economic and strategic interests and pressures so that they are "forced to take account of each other", and those which make a conscious social contract by instituting rules and machinery to make their relations more orderly and predictable and to further certain shared principles and values. Bull expounded this formula to me in the course of our weekend meetings of the British Committee on the Theory of International Politics at Peterhouse, as perhaps the best way of putting the matter. I accepted it then, and still do. It forms a basis for much of the argument in *The Expansion of International Society*[3] which we edited and partly wrote together.

But of course in the real world nothing except a yardstick is exactly a yard long. Well before Bull asked me to join him in editing what became *The Expansion of International Society*, and increasingly once we started work on it, we discussed how the formula applied to actual cases: not marginal ones, but those which were central to our understanding of what expanded and how. Sometimes we resolved our difficulties; but in other cases we still disagreed, or had failed to find a satisfactory answer, when his life was so bitterly cut short.

Europe and the Ottoman Empire

The example which most clearly illustrates the problem in the European states system is the Ottoman Empire. The general position was clear to us. The Ottomans played a major part in the European states system throughout its existence, from its sixteenth-century beginnings to its merger into the present global system as a result of World War One. The trade with the Levant, and through it with further Asia, remained a vital component of the economic life of Europe. Strategically the Ottomans occupied about a quarter of the continent until the end of the seventeenth century. The defeat of the Habsburg bid to establish a hegemonial system in Christian Europe, and the Westphalian settlement (to which Bull attached special importance as the first and decisive formulation of the nature of the European international society) were made possible by Ottoman pressure on the Habsburgs, coordinated by the Franco-Turkish alliance which brought the other anti-hegemonial powers into friendly relations with the Ottomans. Even in the centuries of the Empire's decline the policy of "the Porte" remained a prominent factor in the calculations of the European powers. Yet for most of the period the Commanders of the Faithful disdained membership in the European society of Christian states, and were (perhaps therefore) not considered eligible by the Europeans. They were absent from the settlements of Westphalia, Utrecht and Vienna. Only in 1856, after the Crimean War, were the Ottomans formally accepted into the European international society. Bull's distinction between system and society seemed aptly to fit Ottoman–European relations before and after 1856.

But there the difficulties began. The Turks were not members of what Voltaire called "une grande république partagée en plusieurs états" and Burke "the federative society or diplomatic republic of Europe."[4] But they and the European powers they dealt with did "conceive themselves to be bound by a common set of rules in their relations" and "shared in the working of common institutions." Most characteristic was the institution of capitulations governing trade and residence for Europeans in the Empire. These were as their name indicates a written set of detailed rules, frequently revised: in the period of Ottoman strength the rules were largely formulated by the Ottomans, but as the Empire grew weaker they were increasingly prescribed by the Europeans, as one would expect. The Ottomans also used the machinery of European diplomacy, and in some respects helped to shape it. The Sultans at an early stage accepted resident European ambassadors at Istanbul, though they did not bother to send envoys in return; the European concept of consulates grew out of relations with the Ottomans, and for instance the first English consulate was established at Aleppo; and the spectacle of the diplomatic envoys of Britain and the Netherlands mediating peace between the Holy Roman and the Ottoman empires at the Congress of Karlowitz (1698–99) in order to free the hand of the Habsburgs for the anti-hegemonial struggle against Louis XIV is a classic illustration of the working of a common institution. There was a similar evolution of the codes of conduct that regulated warfare between the Ottomans and their European allies and enemies. Among the grounds listed by Bull in Chapter 1 of *The Anarchical Society* for thinking that states today form an international society, are that "they co-operate in the working of institutions such as the procedures of international law, the machinery of diplomacy and general international organization, and the customs and conventions of war."[5] How far could this also be said of European relations with the Ottomans?

At the beginning of our discussion Bull was inclined to regard Ottoman relations with European states as little more than the relations between states belonging to different international systems which we discussed in our introduction to *The Expansion of International Society*, and to see 1856 as a landmark date when the Ottoman Empire was permitted or obliged to join the European society of states. I on the other hand was more impressed by the intimate involvement of the Ottoman Empire in the European system and by the steady development of rules and institutions to manage and regulate this involvement; so that 1856 seemed to me only one stage in the process, neither the most important nor the last. As we examined the evidence, both of us were impressed by how much the actual conduct of relations between the Ottomans and the Europeans fitted the criteria in Bull's definition of an international society. The working conclusions we reached on the Ottoman issue were fairly close to my original position.

Europe and the Americas

Another major case is the relation to the European international society of the independent European settler states of the Americas after 1776 and during the nineteenth century. They regarded themselves, and were regarded in Europe, as members of the family, though country cousins. They exchanged diplomatic envoys, subscribed to treaties, and towards the end of the period became members of international organizations like the Hague Tribunal. Above all they traded fairly actively with Europe, and the United States also operated in the Pacific. But they all (except sometimes Brazil) kept themselves aloof from involvement in the interests and pressures which formed the nub of the European system, and played no part in European politics; and similarly (except for Napoleon III's intervention in Mexico) the European states, in the full flood of their world-wide imperial expansion elsewhere, left the American states largely to themselves. I suggested at first that the independent states of the Americas could be regarded as belonging to the European society but not the system—the reverse of the Ottomans belonging to the system but not the society. Bull held that according to his formula, membership of an international society presupposed membership of the corresponding system: that the rules and institutions that held a society together were additional to the interests and pressures that made them a system, and in a sense a Toynbeean response to those pressures.

Moreover in fact the American states were members of the European system, economically and in most other ways; they merely preserved a systematic neutrality and non-alignment, like nineteenth-century Sweden and Switzerland and several non-aligned countries today. In the American case, as in many others, I acknowledged that Bull was right. We also recognized that what really and decisively made the settler states of the Americas consider themselves, and be considered, members of the European family was that they were European or European-dominated—in other words the cultural factor, as in the Ottoman case.

Global international society

Another question we discussed was how far in this century membership of the current omnilateral organization—the League of Nations or the United Nations—is a criterion or condition of membership of what we considered to be the present global international society. Both were designed to include all respectable states, deemed worthy of belonging to "the international community"; both were associated with the process of making rules for international conduct; and in general membership involves the activities listed by Bull as grounds for considering that there is a global international society.

The criterion seemed to us unsatisfactory in the case of the League. For most of the twenty turbulent years between the two world wars the four largest and most effective concentrations of power in the system—the United States, the Soviet Union, Germany and Japan—were either not members or took little part in the League's activities. It seemed to us to make little sense to say that between the wars the United States, for instance, had ceased to be part of international society.

The United Nations was designed to correct this inadequacy (I remembered Molotov, during the discussions in the Kremlin in 1945 about the constitution of the new world body, making a slight bow towards the US Ambassador Harriman as he said that the League was scarcely representative of the community of nations). We felt, especially Bull, that UN membership was evidence of membership of international society, though largely symbolic and not absolute. The case of the two Chinas seemed fairly clear. While the regime that controlled the mainland was excluded from the United Nations and not recognized as the government of China by the majority of states, it could be classed as a member of the system but not of the society; and now the regime that controls Taiwan is in the same position. But is the right to occupy the Chinese seat at the United Nations merely a consequence of international recognition, which would thus be the determining factor? And what if, we asked ourselves, a large majority of the members of the General Assembly voted to exclude say Israel, or for that matter the United Kingdom, from that body? Would the excluded state become significantly less a member of international society? Is Switzerland not a member? These

Hedley Bull, states systems and international societies

are questions of theory or semantics rather than practice. The United Nations was not intended to be a criterion or a legislature but a permanent congress of ambassadors representing states that already recognized each other as members of international society; and alas it was difficult to deny that in practice the United Nations was in Abba Eban's phrase "sliding towards marginality", without international society according to Bull's criteria being seriously impaired. We agreed that an international society functions less well for not having an effective omnilateral focus or permanent congress. Especially when a whole lot of new member states feel that such a forum provides one of the few ways of making their views heard, membership helps to keep them within the society (Bull attached much weight to this). But UN membership did not seem a criterion or necessary condition of participation in today's international society.

System, society and culture

These intermittent discussions of specific cases were interwoven with consideration of two more basic questions. Firstly we recognized that the significant divide between the Ottomans and the Europeans was that both sides were conscious of belonging to different cultures or civilizations. How much weight attaches to the cultural homogeneity of an international society, especially our present global one? Secondly, if a group of states, however culturally diverse, is held together by a web of interests and pressures strong enough for us to call them a system, do these very interests and pressures also push the states inexorably into devising the rules and institutions and values in Bull's definition of an international society? These questions need to be examined together.

The extent to which an international society requires a common cultural heritage was linked for us with Heeren's definition of a "Staatensystem." Both of us had a great respect for Heeren. My copy of the first English edition of his seminal *Handbuch der Geschichte des Europaeischen Staatensystems* was given to me by Bull, and one of Bull's last letters to me was about our project to bring it down to the present. Heeren defined a states system as "the union of several contiguous states, resembling each other in their manners, religion and degree of social improvement, and cemented together by a reciprocity of interests."[6] Bull stated in *The Anarchical Society* that this definition differed basically from his own description of a system, "and is closer to what I call here an international society."[7] In fact Heeren's union, requiring what we called common codes of conduct, values, and degree of economic and social development, is much more homogeneous than Bull's society.

The Ottoman case and the present international system showed clearly enough that states involved in what we called an international system need not resemble each other to that extent. But was a common culture necessary for the formation of an international society? The evidence was that up till the present this was always so. For instance the European international society, the parent of our global one, took shape within the compass of Burke's diplomatic republic, and succeeded perhaps because its constituent sovereigns were not merely members of *une grande république* but in most cases related by blood or marriage, so that their wars were family quarrels; and the same was true of the Hellenistic monarchies which Heeren considered the Staatensystem most like his own. Once an international society took shape within a cultural framework its rules and institutions, which reflected that culture, and to a more limited extent even its values, could be exported to states in the system belonging to other cultures, if those states voluntarily (e.g. Japan) or involuntarily (e.g. China) adopted them. A basic theme of *The Expansion of International Society* is that the present global society was formed by the expansion of the European one.

But it was not so straightforward as that. Economic and strategic pressures can and usually do push states from different cultures or civilizations into the same system. The rules and institutions, which states of different cultures in a system work out in response to the challenge and those mechanistic pressures, tend to be essentially expedient and regulatory, designed to give the system order and predictability, like the honouring of commercial contracts, the immunity of envoys and the synchronization of military operations. It is these regulatory arrangements that spread if the heterogeneous system is enlarged. Thus the rules and institutions which the Europeans spread out to Persia and China in the nineteenth century were those which they had evolved with the Ottomans (e.g. capitulations, consulates with jurisdictions over their nationals) rather than those in use within Europe itself (e.g. free movement and residence virtually without passports). In fact neither the Ottoman Empire, nor Persia, nor Morocco, nor China ever really belonged to the *grande république*—Heeren's union—whatever the formal and theoretical position may have been; and even Japan, accepted as an equal ally and a member of the world concert of great powers that asserted collective international authority in China, was not a member. In other words no international system as defined by Bull has operated without some regulatory rules and institutions, and it is hard to see how one could; but that is not enough to call it a society.

This brings us to the second general question about the relation of states systems to international societies. If states locked into international systems evolve regulatory rules and institutions because they cannot manage without, do these rules, and the negotiations which establish them, lead to the acceptance of some common values? (The honouring of contracts and the immunity of envoys are not common values in this sense, but matters of expediency, like saying that honesty is the best policy. Such rules are recognized between communities that maintain only sporadic contact.) A strong case can be made out, on the evidence of past systems as well as the present one, that the regulatory rules and institutions of a system usually, and perhaps inexorably, develop to the point where the members become conscious of common values and the system becomes an international society.

Where does this ethical component come from? In the past common values and ethical norms, unlike regulatory mechanisms, developed and became codified only within a common cultural framework, even though they too might then spread beyond it. For instance in the Greco-Persian system of classical antiquity they developed within Hellas, and in the European case within the *grande république*. When the Europeans, about the middle of the nineteenth century, began to demand that other states which wanted to join their international society should accept some of its values and ethical standards, the criterion they used was the "standard of civilization." Non-European candidates were judged not merely by how they conducted their external relations, but also by how they governed themselves. The insistence on Western values (recognizable as such though of course not always observed everywhere by every Westerner) was a form of collective cultural imperialism, and those who led the historic revolt against the West resented it as much or more than strategic dominion and economic exploitation.

Nevertheless the need for the world-wide international society to have some common values as well as regulatory rules was and is generally accepted. All the members of our present global and multicultural international society actively formulate new values and standards for it. For instance most non-Western states ask for egalitarian economic justice between states, and the second or Soviet-dominated group put forward Marxist criteria, while Western states elaborate human rights for individuals.

We asked ourselves if these ethical standards, whether put forward by Western or non-Western leaders, whether sincerely or in order to promote some material objective, derive essentially from western values, as some maintain. Or has a new modern international culture developed, which determines the life style and the values of the élite statesmen who take international decisions, as others hold? In either case, values and ethical standards would still be developing within a single cultural framework. Alternatively, is the talk about common values empty rhetoric, belied in practice by the actions of the majority of states, in contrast to the reality of the regulatory rules which most states usually do observe? If so, is the world more disintegrated than it was, so that there is in practice no longer an international community? Is it more honest to say that what we have today is no more than a system of states, held tightly together by interests and pressures and organized by rules and institutions comparable to those which regulated European dealings with the Ottomans, but only masquerading as a society? Or is something new happening, comparable to what happened at the Westphalian settlement or after the death of Alexander? Are the states members of our world-wide system consciously working out, for the first time, a set of transcultural values and ethical standards? Bull and I inclined to this optimistic view, but uncertainly. The more we discussed the cultural issue, the more we sensed that there was no easy answer. Our uncertainty is apparent in the last four carefully considered pages of our conclusions to *The Expansion of International Society*.

The same uncertainty besets Heeren's condition that the constituent states of what he called a union should resemble each other in the degree of their social improvement. Our present international society, with its enormous and widening differences of social and material development, falls far short of Heeren's condition. But the desire to bring the whole world up to the same degree of development, and the efforts—such as they are—made by the developed donor states to mitigate the existing differences, suggest that Heeren's condition is felt to be pertinent.

Is it fanciful to see in these arguments and negotiations the dawning of a common consciousness that the new loose international system—which was imposed by the Europeans with their values as well as their regulations, but which has now been substantially disintegrated by the end of Western dominance—needs to take account of principles as well as interests, and to have values as well as rules? And if so, how far will these values be, in Geoffrey Best's language, universally valid but of Western provenance?[8] Or will the disintegration proceed still further, as portents like Ayatollah Khomeini suggest, until the work is made up of a number of *grandes républiques* or unions, linked in a purely regulatory system? The world may be too heterogeneous to become a single *grande république*. But it may become, and is perhaps in the process of becoming, what it scarcely is yet, an international society in the full sense of Bull's definition.

Hedley Bull's distinction between a system and a society is thus a most useful one, not because it causes the complex reality of international relations to be simplified into this category or that, but because it allows that reality to be illuminated by considering it from a particularly productive point of view.

5 The Anarchical Society in the history of international relations: Discussions with Hedley Bull

When I first got to know Hedley Bull, he was a political theorist, interested especially in the international models of systems of states.

He accepted that any group of states so involved with each other that each had to take account of all the others, could be called a system. When such states consciously developed, and in the main observed certain rules, and operated certain common institutions, and perhaps shared some values (though shared values were not essential), they could be considered to have formed an international society.

Martin Wight proposed in meetings of the British Committee that where every state in a system recognized the same degree of independence for all the other members as it claimed for itself, we could call it an international system; but where a few big states had rights and responsibilities that others did not—whether de iure or de facto—we should speak of hegemonial or suzerain systems. Wight and I agreed about the substantial degree of hegemony in the European states system and in the world-wide system which grew out of it. I maintained that in practice every known "international" system had some degree of hegemony; and that the concept of a wholly anarchical society of states was a theoretical absolute that had never been realized.

Hedley Bull, in conversations with me, agreed about the prevalence of some degree of hegemony or imperial authority in historical practice. He said he was not a historian but a political scientist. His point was that nonetheless this concept of a society of fully independent and juridically equal states did exist; and that it played a large part for several centuries in European thought about international relations, and also to some extent their conduct in practice. In particular, the heady era of Western decolonization in which we were then living was dominated by the ideal of a non-hegemonial world society of independent states, to which all remaining colonies ought to accede forthwith regardless of their competence. Hedley as an Australian, regarded the attainment by dependent states of full independence as a natural evolution towards an almost unquestionable goal. Hedley of course, recognized that dependent states might become integral and equal parts of an extended imperial power, as the French, Portuguese and Soviets for instance, proposed.

So it was possible for Hedley, and many others, to regard the propensity to hegemony, which I saw as an integral and ever-present feature of systems of substantially independent states, as an aberration or defect, a failure so far to achieve the more perfect society towards which we were moving. Wight distrusted this belief in Progress. He once observed in this context that to err is human—i.e. that if hegemony was a failure to achieve perfection, it was a permanent failure. But in spite of Hedley's theoretical assumptions, he became, like me, increasingly interested in hegemonial and suzerain systems, and accepted the metaphor of a spectrum from anarchy to empire—from a state of nature to a single universal Leviathan.

Hedley Bull's great book, *The Anarchical Society*, is about the ideal international society and progress towards it. It does not even dismiss hegemony as an aberration, and its index does not include the word. This seemed to him a reasonable limitation for one book. But he was steadily becoming more interested in the historical record—"la storia" itself as Herbert Butterfield liked to call it. He thus came to see the key role of hegemony and anti-hegemonial coalitions in international practice. Understanding and analysing this side of the story was to be my job, and he encouraged me to write about it.

Hedley Bull came to see the origins of the anarchical ideal in the Westphalian settlement of 1648 and the anti-hegemonial coalition that established it. He studied the historical record of that settlement carefully and in detail. In so doing, he saw increasingly how much the realities of seventeenth-century European history differed from what is now often called the Westphalian ideal. But the ideal continued over the centuries to influence practice in many ways. For instance, a main purpose of the rules and institutions of the European international society, from *cuius regio eius religio* to the United Nations, and especially the operation was in Heeren's classic phrase "to protect the weak against the strong." The goal of a free anarchical world of multiple independences, made up largely of emancipated colonies, most notably the United States, effectively relegates hegemony and even more suzerainty from endemic conditions to the very obstacles to be overcome. Or so it seemed to most of us in the 1960s and 1970s. It is my impression that Hedley, especially as he became more historically minded, did not fall into this trap.

Hedley Bull saw that the states which regained their independence from European domination, or acquired it for the first time, accepted the general structure of the world-wide society of states: though it was of Western origin it appeared to the rulers of the new states capable of serving their needs. But otherwise the "third world" that had been assigned subordinate or colonial status by the expansion of the European society of states, seemed to Hedley determined to reject Europe. He intended to write a companion volume to *The Expansion of International Society*, to be called *The Revolt against the*

West, which would show Asia, Africa, Latin America and Oceania as rejecting not only Euro-North American political, administrative and economic standards, but also the West's cultural standards and practices.

In our discussion of this projected volume, I urged him to include the rejection of the Soviet Union by those communist states which were independent enough to do so. Thus of the four major founders of the non-aligned movement, two—Nehru and Nasser—were opposed to British imperialism, and the two others—Chou En-lai and Tito—opposed Soviet domination. But we both realized that we did not know enough about the communist side of the equation to write about it. And of course our discussions took place before Gorbachev and the collapse of Soviet domination.

Hedley seemed to me always somewhat uneasy about the relationship of the newly independent non-white world to Western values and standards of civilization. To many Westerners in the 1960s and 1970s, the decolonization movement and the adoption of universally valid standards of human rights, democracy, the position of women in society, the protection of the environment and so on, went hand in hand. Hedley personally favoured these values as much as any member of the British Committee, including myself. But his understanding of the international situation was that the world was moving towards a society of some 200 substantially independent and therefore culturally very diverse states. The symbolism of the United Nations was the principle of universal membership. Acceptance of a state into the United Nations legitimized membership of international society, and therefore legitimized cultural diversity—a world-wide version of *cuius regio eius religio*.

The international scene has greatly changed since Hedley Bull and I had these discussions. We thought in terms of a global society where we co-existed, and to some extent collaborated with communists and ayatollahs as well as still primitive communities. We did not foresee the collapse in our working lifetimes of bipolarity, or the great technological and military predominance of the United States. But notwithstanding these changes, the Westphalian ideal and Westphalian assumptions remain vigorous and widespread. Most significantly, the long-term assumptions of the United States about a desirable world order remain Westphalian, rooted in their war of independence. And even if, as I asked in my presentation on 5 June, the ideal of multiple and therefore diverse independences turns out to be only a crock of fairy gold at the end of the Westphalian rainbow, still *The Anarchical Society*, and Hedley Bull's work generally, will retain their definitive value in formulating and analysing the concept of a Westphalian world.

More generally, it is well to remember that all ideas do not have the same force. The "unalienable right to life, liberty and the pursuit of happiness", and "liberté, égalité, fraternité" have been *idées notrices* of world political history since their proclamation. And in the more limited sphere of relations between states, the same seems to be true of the Westphalian ideal that Hedley Bull set himself to define.

6 Justice between states

Most discussions of distributive justice assume a distributor. An executive apparatus is presumed, in contemporary terms the State: which will allot goods and benefits among those over whom it exercises authority, and usually also exact contributions from them, according to what "we" decide is just. Formerly distributive justice was determined by the authority of tradition within each cultural pattern, as for instance in the case of inheritance, or by the revelations of divine providence. In the course of time the authority of tradition or providence is called into question while at the same time the capacity of "le pouvoir" to enforce non-traditional decisions on its subjects increases, until in the European case Hobbes could conclude that within a Leviathan state "good" or "bad" may be used to describe only what is defined as such by the ruler. Sometimes and in some places this ruler might combine in a single person both the functions concerned, i.e. the lawgiver who decided what was just, and the executive distributor who distributed and enforced justice accordingly. But it was possible to separate the two functions. This separation underlay the Hildebrandine (clerical) theory of the medieval church and state, the concept of parliament as a legislature, and more modern theories of the general will, the mandate of the majority, etc. Most of the normative rules for distributive justice elaborated by modern academics are in this sense (like much of Plato) cognate variants of the old game of "If I were King." They formulate what is just, and overtly or tacitly presume the other aspect of Leviathan, an executive state apparatus to implement the formula.

It is therefore useful to consider what concepts of justice prevail, and what influence and considerations (or values) shape them, in societies where there is no distributor: societies outside the hide of a single Leviathan. I do not want to consider here the random contacts between primitive monad tribes in a state of nature (surely rather theoretical entities?) but systems and societies of independent states. I want to look at justice *in systematibus civitatum* (the term is Pufendorf's), including what is loosely called international society today.[1]

Without defining each species of the genus, or the marginal cases, we may say that states in a system are independent but also actively interdependent, both in their relations with each other and in the relations between their individual subjects or citizens; and that in the conduct of these relations they recognize, and in the main observe, a set of conventions and rules. These rules are unenforced, except by the power of a group of individual states because there is no supranational executive. They depend for their effectiveness not on consent, as is sometimes claimed, but on their active observance by member states of the system, particularly the more influential ones. (This continual voluntary observance of rules is something quite different from the "just powers" to enforce obedience to the law which the government of a state is said to derive from the consent of the governed; for independent states in a system do not acknowledge the authority of a government over them.) On what corresponds to the legislative side, the member states establish the conventions and rules of an international society or system, and continually elaborate and modify them, by negotiations between executives in a multilateral diplomatic dialogue. Nevertheless these rules have in many systems, including our own, acquired the status of "international law."

The historical evidence indicates that the rules in international systems are usually derived from the traditions of a culture which embraced all or many of the original members, and may have, to a greater or lesser extent, the authority of divine ordinances. This basis is gradually modified by explicit and negotiated conventions. A more useful distinction for our purpose is that between rules which provide a mutual advantage, and those rules and codes of conduct which derive from moral compunction. The stock example of mutual advantage, the immunity of heralds and ambassadors, is virtually universal, even in the most diverse states systems, because it is obviously to the advantage of the ruler or governing body of a state to be able to communicate with the rulers of other states and to hear what they have to say. The stock example of moral compunction is the ban on profaning shrines, which clearly derives from religious scruple although it can be argued that an element of mutual advantage exists here too.

In general the interplay of both elements emerges with particular clarity from the rules regulating war. War is a highly codified form of resorting to force. The conduct in war time of a king and of each individual warrior towards his fellows, his enemies and non-combatants was and still is governed by elaborate rules, which presuppose an individual sense of what is right or just for a warrior to do in various circumstances. This sense is ultimately independent of expediency and of the conduct of the enemy, however much it may be dominated by such mundane considerations in practice. Thus the Moslems in the heyday of their expansion held that the Faithful must spare the lives of non-combatants and of those who surrendered, not because there was any duty to unbelievers, but because this was the conduct which Allah requires of Moslems. The same view was expressed in Spain as "el honor solo es de Dios."

Moreover the reasons for resorting to war (mixed as these may be) are clearly bound up with prevailing concepts of justice. St. Augustine asked "if justice is left out, what are kingdoms but great robber bands?"[2] Indeed war has been regarded in most systems as a last resort when other arguments fail (*ultima ratio regum*), which corresponds to a resort to the law courts between fellow subjects within a Leviathan state. In all systems, and also in other societies which do not acknowledge a common authority, much thought has been given to what constitutes a just war and a just peace. To give two examples in this vast field from the beginnings of our own society. In the early Middle Ages in Western Europe, the Church did not recognize that any resort to war was wholly legitimate, even though the claim itself was just and had been expressly endorsed by the Pope. Thus every combatant on the victorious Norman side in 1066 was required to do penance if he had taken a Saxon life in battle, though the conditions mentioned above were held by the Church to be fully met. St. Thomas Aquinas listed a number of conditions for a just war, including characteristically the condition that it must have a reasonable chance of redressing the injustice at issue, since otherwise it is wrong to sacrifice lives. Similar discussions about how and why a state should resort to war can be found in Confucius, Mencius and the Legalists, who wrote during the period of the Warring States in China, and in similar writings in other states systems. In almost all such writing, and therefore in the minds of those for whom the works were written, the rules—what is just in war and peace—are an amalgam of mutual advantage and moral scruple.

The ethical aspects of *how* to wage a just struggle are not distributive. But when we come to the question of *why*, we find the criteria of a just war and a just peace involve the distribution of territory and other forms of advantage: in other words distributive justice in societies where there is no common sovereign and no distributor.

In such circumstances justice is like the other workings of an international system. It is not a matter of enforcement, or even of consent, but of active observance in practice. It becomes less a matter of high principle than justice inside a Leviathan state and more a matter of adjustment. (A significant word, with implications that should not be despised even within the state.) It must take into account a wider range of considerations than domestic codes.

The classical Greek word *dike*, usually translated justice, meant a broader adjustment when used between one polis and another. What was *dikaion* must take into account what we should call the position in international law, the position on the ground, and the proposal of a mediator (not an arbitrator) acceptable to both sides. It is characteristic of the system that in the fourth century BC the most acceptable mediator was the King of Persia (i.e. his Satrap in Sardis) because Persia was essentially neutral and militarily weaker than the most powerful Greek states, so that the "King's Peace" was what the Persians suggested was *dikaion* after establishing through long negotiations what was most likely to be observed. Dike required that every polis in Hellas should be invited to send delegates to the international congresses held to decide international issues, but not that each should be given an equal voice. (This practice is reflected in Aristotle's dictum that injustice occurs when equals are treated unequally and also when unequals are treated equally. Anaximander came closer to the general concept of *dike* between states with his theory that the fabric of the universe was woven by the interaction of incompatibles, and that *dike* was the process of making good the imbalances caused by the encroachment of one incompatible on another; thus creating an environment in which life, by adaption, could attain its full stature. *Dike* was not something that must be done even if the heavens fall: it was rather what kept the heavens in their place.)

The most remarkable study of the many elements that go to make up the concept of justice between the independent members of the European states system is surely Grotius's *De iure belli ac pacis*. His approach is particularly relevant to our subject, because his aim was to perceive the whole nature of justice in all its manysidedness, both within states and between them in the wider European society. This convoluted and wide-ranging work sets out to record the international practices of his day; to examine their relations to natural law, to tradition, to Judaeo-Christian revelation and to the treaties and conventions between states which established particular rules and settled specific issues; and also to suggest where they might be modified to make them more rational, more *dikaion* (in the sense used above) and more conducive to peace. It is a fascinating attempt to relate the Sein and the Sollen, to establish norms acceptable to God and to princes, to combine theory and experience. Grotius disdained the simplistic theorizing which saw justice as the implementation of a single principle or as deriving from a single source. He seems to have at the back of his mind something like Hooker's concept of "the voice of law as the harmony of the world."

Although the consolidation of the internal power of states, the rise of many vernacular languages in place of common Latin, the Reformation and other divisive tendencies were making Western Christendom a more differentiated society, Europe was regarded by its rulers and statesmen and by its political thinkers as a cultural whole with shared norms and values, until well into the nineteenth century and more significantly as some sort of political community or *res publica*. Burke described Europe in eighteenth-century terminology as a "federative republic" (federative meant linked by treaties). But it was a community without a common government, as Hellas too had been.

The European states system, with its common civilization and shared values, has now expanded into the global states system or international society of today. Although its members are more interdependent than ever, and more keenly conscious of problems which confront us all together and which can be mitigated only by collective action, such as the population explosion, pollution, the destructiveness of nuclear warfare and so on, yet the contemporary states system is more deeply divided than perhaps any previous one. These divisions do not stem today primarily from the differences between Western liberal and Communist governments, although the ideological feud in the days of the Cold War certainly aggravated the differences: Marxist and Western theory and practice both derive from the same European sources, and may be compared to Catholicism and different manifestations of Protestantism during the religious wars (when Grotius was writing). The real differences are due to the expansion of the European system beyond the traditions of the culture which bound together the original members. The majority of the states which are now accepted as members of our heterogeneous international society are culturally and ethnically different from the Europeans (in Europe and elsewhere) who evolved the system, and are increasingly aware of these differences. Moreover most of them were formed from the provinces of colonial empires without any serious tradition or experience of the restraint and compromises required to make an international society work. It is also significant for our purposes that the new members of the international system and most of the older ones have become particularly conscious of issues of justice, and, especially of distributive justice, between states. It has been said that a comfortable majority could be obtained at the United Nations General Assembly for a resolution that to be "justice-loving", in the broad sense used by the majority of the members, is a more important criterion for UN membership than "peace-loving" as stipulated by the Charter.

Now let us assume that in the foreseeable future neither world empire by conquest nor world government by consent will supersede the present system of independent states, which will continue to function as described above. Let us also assume that equality, between states and between individuals in different states, has come to acquire greater moral importance than previously, and is now a value that we consider ought to be enhanced. How can this enhancement be effected?

The arrangement of a greater measure of distributive justice will depend on the sustained and active observance by the members of the system of rules and practices designed to bring this about. These norms will have to be established by patient negotiation, and must carry the approval especially of the more powerful and wealthy states. (UN bodies and similar international organizations are only instruments of multilateral state diplomacy.) If past experience is a guide, moral scruple will not by itself be sufficient for major changes, and there will have to be a substantial element of mutual advantage too. Justice will, as in the past, be less a matter of high principle and more one of adjustment than where there is an effective distributor.

Some objectives of member states like independence and peace (the non-use of force between states) are compatible: their achievement by a state does not deprive others of the same good—on the contrary. But states which seek justice, on their own behalf or on behalf of others, make incompatible demands on the system. If territory of some other form of wealth or advantage is transferred from one state or jurisdiction to another, however justly according to this or that definition of justice, one state will have less because the other has more.

Where such transfers are made voluntarily, because of a change or evolution in the conscience of those who determine the policy of a state—"the free consent of the donor"—no great problem arises for the society of states. But where states disagree about what is just, or about what they are prepared to concede, the conflict must be resolved by resort to force or by the brokerage of the system.

All previous states systems that I have looked at have recognized not only that there will in fact be resort to force, but that the resort to force can be legitimate, if it is designed to correct or prevent an injustice, to right a wrong—in other words, that there is such a thing as a just war. What is just depends of course on the prevailing criterion or norm of justice of the culture at the time.

But—and this is close to the nub of the matter—most states systems, and especially the more civilized ones, have also recognized that justice and just wars should not be allowed to prevail absolutely, regardless of the consequences, whatever the current norm or definition of justice may be. There are and should be other elements in the equation:

a) the attachment of communities to their independence has traditionally been considered the justest of all just causes. (The United States and the Soviet Union are as resolved as the smallest ex-colonial statelet not to allow other states to determine what happens within their domestic jurisdiction.) This attachment sets limits to distributive justice;

b) so does the attachment to peace: which is also a good highly esteemed by civilized states, and is often considered to have a moral value of its own apart from the mundane one of avoiding the suffering and destructiveness of war. Indeed technology may for the first time have made war between major powers (even for justice) unacceptable;

c) at a more practical level, the network of bilateral and multilateral treaties and contractual obligations between states is the necessary foundation of international society; and the obligations which are generally accepted in a states system represent such authority as there is in the absence of a common government. *Pacta sunt mutanda*, no doubt, as the diplomatic phrase has it. But modification by consent is not the same as unilateral disregard: and if a state habitually breaches its treaties and contracts, other states will hesitate to enter into new ones with it. The cause of distributive justice is limited by the implementation of freely accepted obligations, and may suffer seriously from their repudiation;

d) these limitations derive from the compatible objectives of states in a system. There are also more political but nonetheless important ones, such as the balance of power—not the simple journalistic "pair of scales" balance, but the complex "solar system" in which each independent state is a factor in a constantly shifting multiple equilibrium.

44 Justice between states

Moreover the enhancement of equality in the sense desired by progressive opinion in advanced Western societies (from whom the élites of the Third World have largely acquired the argumentation) is not just an issue between states. It is concerned essentially with the more radical concept of equality between individuals irrespective of state boundaries. This concept raises major issues for the negotiation of a series of voluntary transfers of wealth.

A preliminary issue is whether equality means equivalence of consumption by individuals inside the Leviathans in which they happen to be, or involves the right of movement from state to state. Exit visas on demand is a concept dear to Western liberal opinion: the "corollary" of entry visas on demand is usually abhorrent. If we set aside visions of 200 million Chinese turning Siberia into another Manchuria and 200 million East Indians settling in the United States and accept that for the rest of this century at any rate only the lucky few will move and that most underprivileged individuals will have to stay where they are, we come squarely up against the international problem of the consent of the donors.

It is theoretically probable, and factually certainly the case today, that donors will not approve of the way distributors in many recipient states carry out their distribution. The more totalitarian and absolute—the more of a Leviathan—a state is, the harder it will be for any foreign governmental or private donor, or any international agency operating with donors' resources to effect a separate corrective distribution of its own. Three examples will illustrate the point:

a) donors will wish to ensure that what they hand over for distribution in fact enhances equality, and especially that it reaches the poorest in recipient states. Since in a state like Britain wealth from taxation so handed over would otherwise be used to benefit the poorer sections of the British community, trade unionists and the electorate will increasingly object to "taking money from the poor in rich countries to give it to the rich in poor countries." But the élites in less developed countries increasingly insist that aid should be distributed only by their own state agencies. Aid so distributed increases the grip of a government on a country;

b) less developed states which limit their population increase and establish wealth-creating economies increasingly object to "penalizing restraint and development" and subsidizing economic backwardness and the population explosion. Yet once the children are born, it is they who need the help;

c) a more fundamental dilemma is the complaint in the Third World that while the industrial states no longer defend political or economic colonialism, yet "moral colonialism"—the conviction that enlightened opinion in the developed world knows better how less developed states ought to be governed and what forms of justice and freedom ought to prevail there—is more rampant than ever. The most liberal government aid agencies and private foundations seem to the Third World to express sentiments very like the district commissioners and *commandants de cercle* and missionaries of yesterday.

Without belabouring the point further, we may conclude that once we pass beyond the confines and the authority of a single state into international society, it is wholly unlikely that all or a decisive majority of the 150 states that are members of the present system will agree on meaningful and practicable norms of distributive justice: that is, norms which will be implemented through sustained and active voluntary observance by the parties concerned. Proclamations by groups of recipient governments of the norms which they desire make it harder to accept what is available. The complicated and continuous negotiations which now take place between states on approaches to equality are learning to eschew grandiloquence and ultimate objectives, and to confine themselves to modest adjustments which are acceptable to the parties involved and which give due weight to other values. The two most persistent of these other values, independence and the observance of contracts, are both also aspects of what constitutes a just international society.

To sum up on a semantic note. In general it seems to me that our word *justice* tends to acquire too narrow a meaning, and too shrill overtones, to cover the concept we need beyond the state. *Adjustment*, though useful because it implies a shifting equation with many factors, and contains an attractive element of Sein alongside the Sollen, is also too limited and its overtones too flat. *Dike* between city states in Hellas was limited, but at least a mean not an absolute. It comes close to what the treaties of Utrecht called "a just balance" in the European system. In modern English I prefer "what is right and reasonable." The phrase contains the essence of *dike*; it carries on the tradition of discernment in Aquinas and Grotius; and incorporates also Richelieu's *raison d'état* in which right was linked with reason, but extended into *raison de système*. To do what is right and reasonable in the area beyond the state would not cause the heavens to fall, but it would take us quite a distance nearer equality than we are now. And it is easier to reach agreement on what is right and reasonable in international society, and to achieve voluntary implementation of that agreement, than to reach agreement on what is absolutely just.

7 The prospects for a more integrated international society

Where an impersonal network of strategic and economic interests and pressures holds a group of states together, so that the actions of each are partly determined by the actions of the others, we say that they are members of a *system of states*, in the sense that we speak of a solar system. The member states of such systems consciously develop and put into place conventions and rules, and sometimes institutions, to manage the system and increase its order and predictability.

No known states system has existed without some degree of regulation, and it is difficult to see how one could. Where elaborate institutions develop, and some shared values and codes of conduct are present, Western scholars have taken to calling the conscious framework an *international society*. It is a matter of degree, rather than a sharply defined category. For instance, by the seventeenth century the European states had established an international society among themselves. The Ottoman Empire did not belong to that society, although it played a major part in the European system; nor did the Mughal Empire in India or the Manchu Empire in China. Their economic and strategic dealings with the Europeans were regulated by separate agreements, which did not amount to an international society.

However, in the nineteenth century the Europeans (including the United States) brought the whole world into a single economic and strategic system for the first time; and gradually the institutions and to a lesser extent the values of the European society were extended to bring in the non-European states. That complex process Hedley Bull and I tried to describe in *The Expansion of International Society*.[1]

The European international society which expanded with modifications to encompass the world was the result of several centuries of development within the matrix of European culture. Its salient feature, which began to be accepted as the public law of Europe at the seminal Westphalian settlement in the mid-seventeenth century, was the principle that all the member states of the society were, potentially if not always actually, juridically equal regardless of their size and power, and sovereign within their own borders. The European society of states has therefore aptly been called a rulers' or princes' club. Its members were bound together by a fairly tight net of interests and pressures, and by treaty obligations entered into freely or under duress; but it was a club whose members were, or could legitimately claim to be, domestically sovereign and externally equal.

The concept of a society of sovereign and equal states appealed to the non-European states which either reasserted their traditional independence, or acquired it for the first time, as a result of the ebb tide of European dominance and the general decolonization that has now reached its climax with the dissolution of the Soviet Union. The educated elites of these countries resented, personally and on behalf of their people, being treated as inferiors by the Europeans and being told by Europeans how their countries should be administered: whether by an individual power in the case of colonies, or collectively in cases like China. Rulers and governments in particular object today both to any suggestion that their state is inferior and "unequal," and to any outside interference—political, economic or moral—in the way they govern. This is more than an emotional reaction against "neo-colonialism." It is a desire to maintain the salient principle of the European society of states out of which our present global society developed, namely sovereign equality, and to get the West to apply universally this principle which it promulgated. They want to ensure that sovereign statehood is not merely the *constituent legitimacy* of the present international society and of world order, but is respected in practice.

The insistence on an international order based on sovereign statehood and genuine independence is part of the general twentieth-century movement of emancipation from European control. According to this view, collective international action should be taken, where practicable, to remove the last vestiges of colonialism and European (including the United States) domination, for instance in South Africa. But otherwise the less intervention, the less interference in the internal affairs of member states of international society, whether collectively or by an individual great power, the better. In this sense the governments of the non-European states, with few exceptions, want a less integrated international society, as did the members of the victorious coalition that defeated the Habsburg bid for hegemony in Europe in the seventeenth century.

In other words the majority of states today, from the most populous countries in the world like India and China to tiny but sovereign islands, want a non-hegemonial world order. A society of totally independent states is a theoretical absolute, which has never existed in practice. A degree of hegemony is always present in the practical operation of a society. But where the legitimacy of a society is more specifically anti-hegemonial than the practice, as is essentially the case today, the legitimacy of sovereign statehood does restrain the operational practice of powerful states able and inclined to exercise hegemonial authority. It is therefore important to the majority of governments to reaffirm the principle of sovereignty, and to brand hegemonial departures from it as illegitimate. On the other hand the most powerful hegemonial states attach importance to universal principles like human rights and sound economics; and assert their moral obligation to use various forms of pressure and intervention, through international bodies like the United Nations Security Council and the World Bank, to promote these causes.

In the early days of the Cold War between the "first world" of the United States and its Western associates and the "second world" of the Soviet Union and its client allies, four statesmen—Nehru, Chou En-lai, Nasser and Tito—led an international grouping of states that wanted to avoid being entangled with either bloc, and which came to be known as the Non-aligned Movement or Third World. The group adopted a policy of withdrawal from the management of international society. It is significant that two of the four leaders were particularly opposed to British and more generally to Western imperial authority, while the other two were particularly opposed to Soviet dominance. In the succeeding decades almost all the newly independent states established by decolonization joined the non-aligned group, though some of them, like Castro's Cuba and Senghor's Senegal, could hardly be called non-aligned in practice. Non-alignment went beyond external policy, beyond a reluctance or refusal to become entangled as subordinate members in either of the two alliances of the Cold War. It also involved solidarity in the face of the real threat to newly acquired independence, namely the prospect of intervention or irresistible pressure in a Third World state's internal affairs by a leading power or powers in one or the other bloc.

At the present time the constituent legitimacy of sovereign statehood in our global society is threatened by two major trends that militate against it and undermine it. The first is the steady tightening of the impersonal network of economic pressures and interests that makes the system more integrated. The second is the growing pressure of public and media opinion in Western countries in favour of intervention to promote democracy, justice, civil peace and similar moral causes. Both these trends have as great an effect on the integration of the system as the pressure for decolonization during the Cold War had on its loosening.

Economic ties have always played an important role, and usually a dominant one, in the relations between Europe (including the United States and Russia) and the rest of the world. The main driving force of European expansion in the nineteenth century was economic, though other factors such as strategic rivalry and social and religious missionary zeal also played their parts. The mercantilist dogmas that had led to the earlier European wars of the merchants were replaced by the concept of a single world economy. The familiar "shrinking of the planet" has been fostered by technology, and particularly by instantaneous communication, which makes possible the operation of a world-wide market and a single economy; so that the economic life of almost every state is increasingly entangled with the economies of all the others. The global economic system continues its apparently inexorable tightening. For example, the spectacular economic prosperity of many east Asian countries is not autarkic but based largely on exports and imports; and there is hardly a poor state in the Third World that does not rely on trade and aid, in increasingly competitive conditions, to maintain what are often nevertheless dismally low standards of living. The demands of poorer and developing countries for more international aid and markets, and for the management of economic justice, is in effect a demand for closer integration. In order to strengthen their bargaining power, the less developed states co-ordinate their negotiations with international organizations and with donor groups and individual countries, as happens in the Lomé conventions, in OPEC and in the so-called Group of 77 for example. Such institutions and procedures further integrate the practices of international society.

The concept of Non-alignment proclaimed by Nehru and his associates was essentially strategic and political, with moral and emotional overtones of national freedom which also applied to economic decision-making. The concept was eminently suited to that stage of the historical process and the circumstances of the newly emancipated states, as it was to the newly independent states of the Americas in the years following George Washington's call for no entangling alliances. The sharp decline in strategic tension and competition resulting from the end of the Cold War and the dissolution of the Soviet Union has changed the context. The first world and much of the second have come much closer together, to form what may fairly be called a zone of presumed peace, and may perhaps become a single "North." Consequently the relative importance of economic relations and interdependence has greatly increased.

In these different circumstances Cold War labels like the Third World and the Non-aligned Movement seem no longer relevant, though they are retained for reasons of inertia and convenience. New alignments and cleavages are beginning to form. Many governments and scholars, especially perhaps in eastern Asia, are studying ways of conducting the external relations of developing states that are more contemporary and more oriented towards economics. Thus the President of Indonesia, the Chairman of the Non-aligned Movement at the time of writing, advocates replacing confrontation with cooperation in the movement's dealings with wealthy industrialized nations, in order to achieve "common ends" at the world's bargaining tables. But India's voice in this changed world is not yet clearly heard abroad.

When we come to the developed industrial countries of the North, mainly European in race and culture, that made up the first and second worlds of the Cold War—the area from Vancouver to Vladivostok as Gorbachev put it, or more accurately from Oregon to Osaka—we can also see active trends towards a more integrated society. The collapse of the Soviet Union has, on the surface, loosened the ties that held the Western or first world alliance together. The response of all governments and of international institutions like the World Bank and the International Monetary Fund to the tightening net of economic interdependence is still fumbling and uncertain. Strategically and politically, and even economically, the major powers of the North are groping to find new ways of dealing first with each other and then with the rest of the world, and to construct what they call a new world order. As the English school of international relations theory would put it, they are trying to put into place new rules and institutions, codes of conduct, values and ways of thinking, and to modify the traditional ones, in order to adapt international society to changes in the system.

One significant feature of Northern attitudes towards the management of international society is the growing reluctance of the major powers to use force to maintain what they see as order. Not only Germany and Japan, but to a lesser degree other countries including Russia and the United States, are unwilling to send their troops abroad (as opposed to defending their own territories) except as part of a collective peacekeeping or peace-imposing action with United Nations endorsement; and even then there is much public opposition in Northern countries to involvement in such operations. No doubt arrangements will be evolved to provide the forces necessary to keep the peace without allowing them to become merely a means of trying to maintain a rigid status quo. But it seems likely that the pressures brought to bear by the North will be economic rather than military.

Certainly the tightening economic net gives the richer nations greater leverage. But the states of the North do not exploit their economic and technical advantage as ruthlessly as they might. They are restrained by what Herbert Butterfield and Martin Wight called "the principles of prudence and moral obligation which have held together the international society of states throughout its history, and still hold it together."[2] The prudence derives from an awareness of economic interdependence: the moral obligation from long tradition combined with increasing public pressure.

Driven by their public opinions, the governments of the developed Western states try by various means to promote greater economic freedom and private enterprise, greater freedom of speech and opinion, and in general the rights of individuals and minority groups; in short the rights of citizens of less developed states against their governments. Indeed many pressure groups in the United States and some in Western Europe object to rich industrialized countries defending their material and strategic interests (what used to be called their national interests) by bringing pressure to bear on less developed ones. These groups want the developed states to exercise pressure "altruistically and not selfishly", by denying aid, applying trade sanctions and excluding recalcitrant states from international organizations, and if possible collectively but if not then unilaterally, to promote human rights and justice as liberal opinion in the West understands these terms. There is a growing sentiment that in a shrinking world made more visible by television we are all fellow citizens, and that concern for the welfare of the less fortunate should not stop at a state's borders. This perception is, of course, the opposite of the basic rule of the princes' club and of the constituent legitimacy of our decolonized international society, that governments should not interfere in each other's domestic affairs.

The prospects for a more integrated international society 51

The standards of behaviour laid down by the West for the conduct by governments of their domestic affairs are thus not intended to be selfish or imperialist, and they apply impartially to all members of the society. They correspond to the "standards of civilization" on which the European powers insisted during their nineteenth-century expansion, well described in Mr. Gerrit Gong's book.[3] What was then called civilized domestic behaviour is now called democracy and a respect for human rights. One must expect pressure of this kind from powerful developed countries to increase, and to find a louder echo among the dissatisfied elements of targeted states. In the face of these demands by the North, and the changing climate of world opinion on these subjects, other governments are finding it increasingly necessary to maintain what Americans call standards of governance that partially meet the demands of donors and trading partners while retaining domestic autonomy in their own hands.

The impersonal pressures of a contracting system and the increasing tendency to influence the domestic practices of states has caused growing doubts about the continuing validity of sovereign statehood. How far can different aspects of statehood—economic policy, defence, human rights—be determined in practice by hegemonial great powers or international bodies like the World Bank, or delegated to a confederation (a prominent issue in Europe), without destroying sovereignty and independence? Or, as I formulated the question in *The Evolution of International Society*,[4] will "the modern successors of the European princes find themselves constrained by the pressures of a tightening system and by the institutions and practices of a more integrated society to act increasingly in ways that deprive them of independence de facto, externally and internally, . . . while leaving intact the symbolic legitimacy of the state and varying degrees of real autonomy?"

The great movement of disintegration of the European empires into multiple independence that began with the American Revolution of the 1770s and reached its climax in the half century from the independence of India and Pakistan in 1947 to the breakup of the Soviet Empire in 1990, led to a political and strategic loosening of international society. Let us accept that the tide is now running the other way again, and that this loosening may have started to yield to a more closely knit international society in which the sovereignty of the member states will matter less, emotionally and in practice; and that the net of the system will continue to tighten. What might a more integrated society, whose institutions and practices correspond to a tighter system, look like? An answer to this question can only be an informed guess, based on the evidence of the past and on present trends so far as we can observe them.

First, the history of international societies shows that when a system of states became tighter because the pressure of interdependence increased, the practice of the society, that is the ways of applying its rules and using its institutions, became more hegemonial. Sometimes the hegemony was exercised by a single power with some anti-hegemonial resistance, and at other times there was a diffused hegemony of a group of great powers such as those that ran the Concert of Europe after the Napoleonic empire. If our present international society becomes more integrated, it is likely to be managed in practice by a diffused hegemony based on such coordination as the leading industrial powers can achieve.

But secondly, the rules and institutions will surely retain the constituent legitimacy of independent sovereignty, in many cases recently achieved and still precious; and the legitimacy will temper the exercise of hegemonial management. The legitimacy of sovereignty is enshrined in and symbolized by the omnilateral United Nations. Since the end of the Cold War the leading powers of the world have shown a greater willingness to work through the United Nations on strategic and peacekeeping measures. The five permanent "veto" powers consult among themselves and with the other most interested parties, and then use the UN machinery to implement their decisions. The end result is not unduly dictatorial. It is not necessary for the five powers to agree. As in similar past systems, acquiescence is a formula that enables a major power to maintain its principles and yet to allow collective action. The need to avoid a veto and to secure an adequate quorum of support from other states usually ensures that UN action is broadly acceptable. If the composition of the Security Council is altered to reflect the influence of Germany, Japan and India, as is now under discussion, the effective decisions may become harder to reach but more widely acceptable. Many smaller states, and a large part of Western public opinion, would like to see the United Nations able to act more effectively to maintain international order and security.

Thirdly, in contrast to the virtually equal representation of all states, great and small, in the United Nations, international economic and financial institutions like the World Bank and the International Monetary Fund are formally weighted according to the economic strength of the members, and in practice reflect especially the views of the donor states. In this increasingly important sphere of international action the major economic powers such as the Group of Seven maintain a continual consultation on the policies which they will implement together, or at least not oppose, acting through the appropriate international bodies. Most of the developing states, for their part, seem likely to follow the example and leadership of their most economically successful members, whose prosperity and living standards already equal those of many states of the North. Within this hegemonial economic framework the familiar conflicts of interest, between producers and consumers of commodities and technology, lenders and borrowers of capital, will continue. The common ends of which President Soeharto speaks will be achieved through a long series of negotiated bargains and compromises.

Indian policy as conducted by the Nehru family in the period of the Cold War and decolonization was remarkably successful both in establishing broad principles in the international field and in the tactics of strategic and economic negotiation. Serious thought is now being given by Indian scholars and practitioners to the new role which their country should play in a much changed world: this book is one example. There are therefore good grounds for hope that in the coming decades India will make a contribution to a changed world order which is commensurate with its size, its millennial civilization, and its intellectual, economic and military capacities. In particular, India may find ways to adapt the principles of non-hegemonial statehood and political independence to a more integrated international society where collaboration replaces withdrawal. Indian statesmen may be able to induce other governments to achieve standards of internal governance comparable to Indian democracy and respect for human rights, and thus to preserve the principle of independence and a substantial autonomy in practice. In so doing India may also be able to provide more effective advice and leadership than in the past to the large number of smaller, poorer states that are much less capable of development or of finding by themselves acceptable places in a reorganized international society.

8 "The Practice Outruns the Theory"

I would like to examine the general maxim that the rules and institutions of an international society are more fixed than the practice, with particular reference to the contemporary scene. I am here concerned with what can loosely be called the theoretical or constitutional legitimacy of an international society, not academic theories about the nature of such societies. Practice is fluid and experimental, inclined to improvise and to look for the expedient Those practices and arrangements which work—which seem to the leading participants to pay dividends—are then continued and become codified. What is at fast simply conduct can become a code of conduct. There get to be interpretations of rules, and new uses for institutions, which modify the original purpose; and these revisions gradually became accepted as part of a new conventional legitimacy. This is a general rule: of course, there are exceptions.

One result is that a serious gap can occur between the constitutional legitimacy of an international society—what Hedley Bull calls its rules and institutions—and its practice. People become aware that what happens on the international scene does not correspond very closely with what is supposed to happen. This discrepancy can cause unease, a sense of illegitimacy, a resentment of usurpation, especially by the practice of the most powerful members of the society. In all international societies practice feels obliged to innovate, to deal with new circumstances; but the more the practice appears to conform to the accepted legitimacies, the less unease and resentment there will be.

I discuss the role of legitimacy in the operation of international societies in my book *The Evolution of International Society*. May I quote the following summary from the conclusion.

> Legitimacy in the ancient world was the oil that lubricated the operative machinery of a society. The more its rules and institutions were considered legitimate, the more easily it could change its practices. The experience of the European society confirmed the lubricating role of legitimacy; but it also showed how the anti-hegemonial legitimacy established by the Westphalian settlement and explicitly confirmed by Utrecht could operate as a check on the swing of the pendulum as it was

designed to do. Even so, where the pressures for change were great, practice disregarded legitimacy, or found a way round it; and over a period the legitimacy adjusted to take account of the practice. In the contemporary world the rules and institutions (notably the United Nations) and the nominal values of our international society give a stamp of legitimacy to a very high degree of multiple independence. Even the strongest powers profess to respect the independence of all members; and this reassurance makes the hegemonial reality more acceptable.

Two historical examples

International societies differ from one another, but they have certain resemblances or common characteristics. It may, therefore, be useful to take a brief look at two familiar historical examples. First, the imperial authority of Augustus and his immediate successors. Second, the functioning of the European international society during the hegemony of Louis XIV.

Augustus came to power as a result of victory in civil war, and was constitutionally, if one can use such a term, the last of a number of usurpers of the legitimate authority of the Roman senate and people. In practice, he was a monarch, regulating in different ways the heterogeneous conglomerate of territories that we call the empire—which ranged from client monarchies like Herod and theoretically sovereign allies like Athens to directly administered provinces. He operated largely through his private staff, and most of the expenditure involved came from his personal coffers: especially from Egypt, which he ruled as a private domain. In the east, he allowed himself to be worshipped as divine, like the Hellenistic Kings. But, at Rome, he was careful to observe the republican forms. He refused titles like rex and Romulus, and called himself just a senator, first among equals (a contradiction in itself); the offices of consul and tribune of the people continued nominally, but in his own or other safe hands; and he had his decisions ratified by the cowed senate. The different expedients were deliberately ambiguous but they were not a farce: they made his rule easier for others to accept, both at Rome and in the east, and, therefore, for him to exercise.

The international society established by the seminal settlement of Westphalia in 1648 was resolutely anti-hegemonial, devised and imposed by the victorious coalition against Habsburg hegemony. If I may speak in broad generalities, the new society consisted of states which were recognized as independent and those which were in practice able to act as such. The governments of these states were to treat each other as de facto equals, based on new concepts of international law, and to refrain from interference in each other's domestic affairs (especially in matters of religion). The makers of the Westphalian settlement recognized the need for international order: the order which they promulgated was anti-hegemonial, as opposed to the hegemonial order which the Habsburgs envisaged and to some extent operated. It was one of those brief periods of mirage, like the peacemaking after World War One "the war to end war", and the great decolonization of the 1960s and 1970s—periods when, as Xenophon said about the defeat of the Athenian empire, men thought that all Hellas might be free. But the mirage soon gave way to the reality of Louis XIV's hegemony. Louis was half a Habsburg with a Habsburg wife, and he aimed in practice to impose a new hegemonial order. He controlled the Habsburg position of Holy Roman Emperor through a German client princeling, and replaced the Vienna—Madrid axis of his cousins with a Versailles—Madrid axis. But he operated as far as possible within the framework of Westphalia: enlisting the other victor allies, using the techniques of subsidy and diplomacy developed by the coalition, and the Westphalian arguments of legitimacy and international law. So his hegemonial practice outran the new anti-hegemonial theory, but made itself more acceptable by operating through and under the cloak of the Westphalian legitimacy.

The contemporary international society

The same is true of our contemporary international society. To start with the legitimacy. The contemporary society is nominally very loosely organized: even more so than the European society after Westphalia, and much more so than the system of Augustus. It is theoretically predicated on some one-hundred-and-eighty plus independent sovereign states, linked by such omnilateral institutions as the United Nations and international law. Both international law and the United Nations assume that sovereign states are equal de iure: as Emerich de Vattel said, a dwarf is as much a man as a giant. The sovereigns accredit ambassadors to each other and to international organizations on a basis of equality (with a few exceptions like the five permanent members of the UN Security Council). This sovereign independence and equal membership of "international society" was much emphasized during the decolonization of the European seaborne empires (circa 1947–77), and is particularly prized by those formerly dependent states which have acquired or regained their independence as a result of the decolonization process and now make up a majority of independent states. Moreover, it is a society in which the internal affairs of a sovereign member state are, except as provided for in treaties freely signed, in theory its own business, as has been the case since Westphalia. Article 2/7 of the United Nations Charter still debars that body from discussing anything that is wholly or mainly the internal concern of a member state. According to the *New York Times* of 30 January 1992, for instance, "China, India and some of the third world nations on the Council are resisting any ringing endorsement of such goals as safeguarding human rights and promoting democracy, arguing that by doing so the Council would be involving itself in the domestic affairs of other [sic] countries." Also, where security and the protection of the weaker against the stronger are concerned the basic rules of our society deal mainly with strategic security and immunity from external coercion, and much less (though increas-

"The Practice Outruns the Theory" 57

ingly) with collective economic security and the management of international economic activity.

The theory, the legitimacy, has long included the concept of dependent states, such as colonies, which may be legally distinct from the imperial state (such as Hong Kong, la Nouvelle Calédonie), and territories in dispute between two sovereign states, under the occupation of one of them (the Kurile Islands, Peruvian/Ecuadorian Amazonia, the Golan Heights). But it is uncomfortable with theoretically independent states which are clearly dependent in practice. Thus, it balks at the actual situation on the ground of the Lebanon (controlled mostly by Syria and a small part by Israel); Panama; the ex-Soviet republics of Central Asia (military and economic relationship with Russia); ex-French tropical Africa; and other examples. The situation in Palestine (the West Bank and Gaza) is particularly awkward. Perhaps the most glaring example in recent times was the Soviet satellite states of Eastern Europe, which were in theory independent member states of international society but in practice scarcely sovereign at all.

Those examples are not exceptions. They illustrate the truism that the actual practice of the contemporary international society is very different from the theoretical legitimacy.

Let us look, first, at the reality behind the theoretical equality of states; then, at the reality of intervention, with special reference to individual human rights; third, at economic security and aid, and finally at the general concept of sovereignty.

Equality of member states

In our current international society all independent states, or at least all members of the United Nations are treated as juridically equal, in international law and in such minor matters as the precedence accorded to ambassadors. But in practical terms the familiar difference between the strongest and the weakest states is truly immense. We might discuss the following aspects.

The discrepancy between the power of the different members of any international system, and consequently their influence in it, is obvious and inevitable. The influence of a member state in the system is determined not only by its size (both area and population), wealth (a very different criterion, note Singapore and Saudi Arabia), degree of development etc., but also by its purposefulness, experience in statecraft, and more subjectively its reputation and tradition, and the way in which its capacities and intentions are perceived by others. Therefore, we find that in all known systems the effectiveness of the members, meaning all the above variables taken together, varies very widely. Moreover, the strongest and most effective members exercise a degree of hegemony, some sort of authority explicit or tacit in the system. Hegemonial authority may be exercised by one very powerful state (e.g. Louis XIV), by a diarchy of two collaborating states (e.g. the Athenians and Spartans after the Persian wars), or collectively by a group of great powers (e.g. the Concert of Europe after the Napoleonic wars). Hegemonial authority carries with it privileges but also responsibilities, and derives additional advantages by making the exercise of hegemony acceptable to other members of the society. This is what Butterfield and Wight meant by "the principles of prudence and moral obligation which have held together the international society of states throughout its history, and still hold it together."[1]

In our present society, the discrepancy in power is unusually large. The process of decolonization not only re-established Asian and Mediterranean states with millennial traditions of civilization and statecraft, but also made a host of independent but small and undeveloped mini-states from what de Gaulle unkindly called "the dust of empires." It is true that an analogous situation existed after Westphalia, when many of the basic principles of the European international society were established. At that time, a number of minor princelings in the Holy Roman Empire had become independent in practice if not yet absolutely in theory. But the analogy, though useful, is not very close: the princes of the Empire and governments of city states like Hamburg were on average as capable, and their realms as "developed", as the larger members of the seventeenth-century European society, so that Voltaire could reasonably describe it as, "une grande république partagée entre plusieurs états"; whereas the same is manifestly not yet true of the inexperienced "dust of empire" states.

Consequently, the hegemony in our contemporary society is constitutionally tacit rather than explicit, and runs counter to a literal interpretation of the equality of member states; but it is generally acknowledged in practice. The pattern of two antagonistic superstates with rival hemispheres of influence came to an end with the collapse of the Soviet Union, and we now have only one state with a global reach. President Bush in his last State of the Union address put it bluntly: "A world once divided into two armed camps now recognises one sole and pre-eminent power, the United States of America." But though America is temporarily the only superpower, it is not in a position to exercise a single hegemony—to manage international society by itself. First, it needs the cooperation of other "great powers." This need is especially apparent in all activity short of the actual use of force, where what matters is economic clout, what Diane Kunz calls the importance of having money. The two most important centres of economic power whose collaboration is needed to make an effective world economic concert are Japan and Germany (which is now merging itself into a united Western Europe). Second, if America is not to rely on unilateral pressure, which would be both destabilizing and beyond its strength, and if the exercise of managed authority is to be broadly acceptable to the other members of international society, the decisions of the great power concert need to be implemented through legitimate and constituted channels: particularly the machinery of the United Nations, and multilateral economic organizations like the World Bank and the International Monetary Fund. In other words, it will pay the concert to operate in accordance with the legitimacies.

I, therefore, think that we should recognize the world, not as a hierarchy of states or a suzerain system, but as an international society managed to some extent by a group of great powers. This pattern is somewhat similar to the nineteenth-century concert in Europe (in which incidentally the five great powers often disagreed, but managed to collaborate or acquiesce often enough to make the concert system work). During the forty years of the Cold War, the United States was the leading state of the non-communist world, both strategically and economically, and indeed the only global power. If, today, that eminence is eroding, the association of post-communist Russia as a partner, and the growth of Japan and the West European Community, makes a hegemonial concert perhaps the most likely form of successful management of our international society.

Intervention and human rights

The milder forms of hegemony are usually concerned only with the management of the inter-state aspects of a system. A hegemonial power (or powers) will induce, or in extreme cases compel, other members of an international society to modify their external behaviour to the extent necessary to conform to hegemonial management. For the most powerful state (or directorate of states) to go further than this, and to exercise significant control over the *internal* affairs of other member states, may be called dominion rather than hegemony. The legitimacy of an international society may draw a clear dividing line between the two—that is between inducing members to conform to the society's rules and institutions (which the most powerful members interpret, and may have written) on the one hand, and interference in the internal affairs of members on the other. But the line is notoriously difficult to draw in practice. There is a large grey area of pressure and interference which the interveners justify by the argument that internal developments such as building up a war machine, and especially weapons of mass destruction, affect what is currently called international peace and security, i.e. the orderly management of the system. (The justification is often quite reasonable, but sometimes amounts to casuistry.)

In any case, interference on the grounds of religion, ideology, or in this century the pattern of economic life (discussed below), have been regular practices, especially in times of hot or cold war. There is also a long tradition, one might almost say a norm, of intervention by outside powers in civil wars, overtly and covertly, collectively and by individual foreign states. Collective intervention, and intervention by a single powerful state or group of states acting with the explicit endorsement or tacit consent of the collective institutions of the society (e.g. the Gulf War), are not contrary to the legitimacy. But assigning degrees of legitimacy is usually a secondary issue in the practice. The practical problem with the civil war in Angola, for example, was to manage and contain the various interventions and to negotiate an end to hostilities with the leading interveners, which included both superpowers. The practical problems connected with the spread of nuclear weapons and related subjects are more obviously interventionist, but have acquired a certain legitimacy of their own.

In our contemporary society, the Western powers also apply pressure, though less systematically, to ensure minimum standards in the observance of human rights of individuals against their own government. The relationship of a sovereign to his subjects has traditionally been the most quintessentially internal business of a state. The insistence by Western governments on human rights in other states now goes very far: for example, the United States makes a declaration on the subject a condition of diplomatic recognition of successor states of the Soviet Union. But the Western media and large sections of public opinion demand a still stronger attitude. The insistence on human rights is a modern version of the nineteenth-century insistence on a standard of civilization in non-European states wishing to be admitted to the European-controlled international society.[2] China, now as a century ago, plays a leading role in active opposition to demands by the most powerful members of the international system; but the Chinese government's attitude may once again be a rearguard action. Human rights, and the wider issues in international relations which can be subsumed under the rubric "the Diplomacy of Justice" (on which Professor John Vincent was compiling a book when he tragically died), illustrate how far certain aspects of contemporary international practice outrun the theory.

Economic security and aid

The economic fabric of contemporary international society is perhaps the clearest illustration of the gap separating its practice from the concept of some one-hundred-and-eighty plus sovereign states all free to run their own domestic economy as they see fit. In an absolute sense, independent governments can exercise this right; and most members of international society do so to some degree. A few states practise autarchy. Some others have resources like oil which enable them to live comfortably, if they or foreign experts produce and export it. But in practice the majority of members are unable at present to generate by themselves the standard of living which their populations have come to expect. To achieve even low standards, they must import both the great range of goods which they can make only at unreasonable expense or not at all, such as electric light bulbs and surgical equipment, and also educational and other managerial services; and this is beyond their unaided means. The problem is often compounded by rapid population increases. Most of the populations, and, indeed, most responsible administrators, of the Less Developed Countries (LDCs) are more concerned with poverty, that is with economic insecurity, than with the threat of foreign invasion and conquest, that is with strategic insecurity.

"The Practice Outruns the Theory" 61

What, in theory and in practice, are the rich states required to do about the plight of the poorer ones? The notion that the great powers or superpowers in an international society are responsible for the security of the weak is part of *raison de système* and, of course, not new. Thucydides has the Corinthians tell the Spartans: "The true author of the subjugation of a state is not so much the immediate agent as the state which permits it though it could prevent it, especially if that state aspires to the glory of being the liberator of Hellas." Heeren claimed that the obligation to preserve the balance of power was that it protects the weak against the strong. Woodrow Wilson championed the alternative concept of achieving collective strategic security for the weak by means of a league of well-intentioned great powers. But this is surely the first time in history that the economically most developed states have recognized any obligation to supplement the economic and social capacities of weaker states?

International economic responsibility involves the recognition by the economically stronger states that it is in the interest of all the members of an international system that the pressures and constraints caused by their inescapable involvement with one another should be managed as effectively as possible. In other words, it adds a new dimension to the extension of *raison d'état* to *raison de système*. A massive and complex aid programme of bilateral and multilateral government aid provides the LDCs with grants, loans, preferential import regulations, an array of technical experts, and educational and other opportunities. This governmental aid is supplemented by a considerable volume of private investment: which most recipients, from Russia to small Pacific and Caribbean islands, are eager to obtain, in spite of neo-colonialist arguments and many cases of unjustifiable exploitation. A recent Foreign Office enquiry showed that British Embassies and High Commissions in some LDCs were spending up to 80 per cent of their work time on questions connected with aid. Certainly, this aid is in the enlightened self-interest of the donors, as was the Marshall Plan. It is also true that the aid and investment of resources and know-how falls far short of the capacity of the recipient states to usefully absorb it; and that there are various limits to what the donors will do: the resources available, the willingness of democracies to spend abroad resources needed for under-privileged voters at home, and the donors' inexperience of what aid achieves a desired result. Nevertheless, the concept of the responsibility of the economically strongest states (or confederacies) for *collective economic security* exists and is being partially implemented in practice. It is also steadily becoming part of the legitimacy. We might discuss the implications for the society of states.

We should also note that the aid is largely decided and administered hegemonially. International financial organizations operate not on the basis of one member one vote but according to the member's contributions giving the United States and other leading donors a hegemonial say. The World Bank and the International Monetary Fund, as well as the collective hegemony of the Group of Seven, put what is often severe pressure on recalcitrant recipient members to allow a market economy, to show fiscal prudence, to pay some interest on debt, etc. In practice, the conditions set by donor governments and international organizations amount to a degree of control over the domestic economies of recipients. This is not, legalistically speaking, intervention in the internal affairs of member states: it is simply the price of the collective economic security which the weak countries ask for. And, of course, recipient governments, and their sympathizers in rich democracies, demand more aid with less strings. But, in practice, the scope and scale of economic aid is determined by the donors, like so much else in international society.

Sovereignty

On the subject of sovereign independence generally, let me submit for discussion two paragraphs from my book mentioned above.

> The European concept of sovereignty... as its name implies, was an aim of rulers and princes, who wanted to be masters over all their subjects but to acknowledge no master over themselves. The concept of sovereignty protects the weak prince against the strong. The sovereignty to which Westphalia committed the European society of states was essentially domestic. What a sovereign did in the territories recognized as legitimately under its government was not the business of other sovereigns. In principle sovereign princes and states were also free to act as they saw fit in their external relations. Indeed the ability to conduct an independent foreign policy was widely regarded as the test of genuine sovereignty. But the relations of a sovereign state with the other members of the sovereigns' club were constrained by the pressures of the system and by the rules and codes of conduct of the society, and also most of the time by a degree of hegemonial control.[3]
>
> The awareness that states are being constrained into a tighter system, especially in the economic field, has led to increasing doubts about the continuing relevance, and even the reality, of independent sovereignty. The real sovereignty of the *stato*, established by Italian and German princes and maintained by the princes' club and the romantic nationalists, remains precious, especially to the governing elites of states recently emancipated from imperial rule. But the external and internal freedoms of action associated with independent states no longer seem to be bound together into a monolithic whole. In the rhetoric of statehood, the different elements in the bundle—from defence and immigration to currency and human rights—can be assigned to various confederal or society-wide bodies without destroying the identity and ultimate sovereignty of the state. Or to put it more prosaically, the modern successors of the European princes find themselves constrained by the pressures of a tightening system and by the institutions and practices of a more

integrated society to act increasingly in ways that deprive them of independence de facto, externally and internally, so that their governments no longer control a *stato*; while leaving intact the symbolic legitimacy of the state and varying degrees of real autonomy.[4]

In a tightening system, the more the symbolic independence of the member states can appear to continue, and the greater the genuine autonomy allowed to the member states by the hegemonial managers of the society, the easier and more acceptable the practice of the society will be.

Concluding Questions

The practice of our present international society has outrun its ostensible legitimacy. I must leave the reader with the following questions.

1. It is now:

    a) how much more hegemonial and less "equal"?
    b) how much more interventionist, especially about human rights?
    c) how much more committed, in practice and in theory, to collective economic security?
    d) how much less sovereign?

2. In which directions is innovative practice moving?
3. How is legitimacy adjusting to practice?

9 The future of the Westphalian anti-hegemonial system

> Unpublished paper read at the ISA meeting at the University of Twente, Netherlands, 2000

The purpose of this paper is to address the following set of interconnected questions:

1. Is globalization in the economic sector undermining the basic territorial principles of the Westphalian system?
2. Does the combination of postmodern states at the core and failed states at the periphery point to the emergence of a post-Westphalian international system, and if so what are its characteristics likely to be?
3. How much of the Westphalian system of law, political principle and symbols will be swept away and how much is likely to survive?

It is not given to man to foresee the future with any clarity of detail. It is embarrassing to read the predictions about international relations written twenty, or fifty, or one-hundred years ago. Those predictions were unable to foresee major specific events. For instance, in the early 1980s how many foreign offices or defence ministries, how many pundits, foresaw the imminent collapse of the Soviet Union and the break-up of the Russian empire? In fact, although the nature of the international system can change with startling discontinuity, almost all such forecasts are little more than projections and extrapolations of the present and the recent past. Therefore when trying to discern the future we must feel our way cautiously, and keep ourselves from merely parroting the fashionable ideas of our time.

But if we step back and allow ourselves a longer perspective, we can also discern, in addition to the wide range of unpredictable specific events, some long term trends which are carried forward by their own momentum. These trends have continued even through such great events as two world wars and the rise, expansion and collapse of Soviet power. We need to note the impact on Westphalian orthodoxy, and on current practice, of three interconnected long term trends. First, decolonization or the granting of nominal independence to a large number of weak states on the periphery of the system—states which cannot make that independence real. Second, the resurgence of Asia. Third, the growth at the core of a sense of collective responsibility for what happens in the periphery.

Westphalian theory

What, then, is the present system from which our enquiry must start? The system that we call Westphalian is based on two main premises. First, states are members of an anarchical society, meaning that there is no overarching authority over them. And second, all states are at least juridically and morally equal. A third premise, that a group of people who want to become independent have a right to do so, is less absolute. These basic premises pose the question: what are the qualifications for acceptance as a member state? One way of describing the postulates on which we try, or pretend, to operate the international system can be described as follows (I borrow largely from a description suggested to me by George Kennan):

- Every group of people that conceives itself, or whose leaders conceive it, as a nation ought to be given the quality of a state, and recognized as such on a basis of equality with all other states.
- Every state deserves to enjoy unlimited sovereignty and independence; and no other state or international organization should interfere in its internal affairs.
- A world consisting solely of such states, with no other permissible status, constitutes a firm and sufficient structure for a global international society now and for the indefinite future.

The structure of the neo-Westphalian international society is held to assume concrete shape in the United Nations.

The unreality of these postulates is obvious, as is the great gap between them and what actually happens in the world, and indeed in the United Nations. Of course states are not all even remotely alike. That is what Inis Claude calls the peas in a pod fallacy. The concept of a system in which all the member states are equally independent is a theoretical point of infinity: it does not exist in practice.

I want to offer some justifications for the following answers to the questions quoted at the beginning of this paper. I want to consider whether these answers are likely, not whether they are desirable.

1. The basic principles of the Westphalian order are inadequate to deal with the modern world. Economic globalization is one factor in this obsolescence, but not the only one.
2. A post-Westphalian system is slowly and fitfully emerging in practice, based on a concert of hegemonial great powers at its core, and a large periphery of other states with very varied degrees of dependence. Peripheral states will continue to become increasingly willing to accept the donors' terms for the aid they need.

    The concert will operate its hegemony where practicable within the existing framework of multiple independences etc., which preserves the self-respect and the limited autonomy of the peripheral states.

66 *The future of the Westphalian anti-hegemonial system*

3. More generally, state independence is becoming more limited and supranational authority more acceptable. "Nation-states" everywhere may cease to command total sovereignty and undivided allegiance, as is already starting to happen in Europe.

The two hundred or so member states of the present international society vary enormously in character, and in size, wealth and authority. Each of the great concentrations of power like the United States, Western Europe, Russia, Japan and increasingly China and India, have more than ten-thousand times the wealth and authority of the smallest and weakest. About half of the members are what the questions at the beginning of this paper call "failed states at the periphery", or at least ministates and quasi-states, dependent on outside help of various kinds. And the flip side of this dependence is the hegemonial strength and authority of the largest and richest states.

It is a cliché that the technological revolution continues to make the world shrink. Today no state is as independent as political rhetoric and part of the academic literature claims. (There has been greater change in Europe than elsewhere, both in the theory and in the practice. Many Europeans now consider sovereign independent nation states obsolescent: Chancellor Kohl called them "vollkommen überholt.") In fact we are living in a constricting international system. States are held together, first, by the impersonal and ever-tightening net of interests and pressures (trade, technology, weaponry, ecology) that forces us all into closer interdependence. Second, states further bind themselves with the rules and institutions which they consciously put in place to manage the interests and pressures of their enforced interinvolvement. These constitutional provisions—international law, diplomacy, the United Nations and so on—are at present permeated by neo-Westphalian concepts. Third, the operation of the system is largely determined by its most powerful members, or in other words by hegemonial authority. Hegemony is compatible with the letter of a Westphalian order, but not with its spirit.

A short look back

Before we look at how the present phase of the system functions and how it may project itself into the future, we need to take a look back (as Buzan and Little say). We should note how we got to where we are, and especially how certain long term trends developed the momentum they now possess.

Hegemony is a large subject. It has taken many forms in the recent past. The long term trend towards collective hegemony—an effective core—in the system goes back two centuries. It began with the nineteenth century Concert of Europe. That Concert met one of the essential conditions of success: it included all the effective great powers in the system. To maintain peace and order and impose its values (some of which we no longer share), the Concert powers felt not so much a right as an obligation to intervene in other states, first in Europe and then in the global periphery, contrary to the Westphalian principle of non-intervention. Europe was not free from armed conflict between Concert powers in the mid-century; but from the Vienna settlement of 1815 to the collective intervention in China of 1900 (which included the United States and Japan) the Concert functioned as the loose central core of the European international society as that society expanded to cover the whole world. A post-Westphalian system began to take shape within the framework of the Westphalian rules and principles.

After the anarchy of the two world wars, another abrupt change ushered in forty years of the Cold War. Two rival hegemonies, US and Soviet, were locked together by the very real strategic struggle against each other and by the shell of neo-Westphalian institutions that encompassed the two hegemonies and the "non-aligned" world. Since the collapse of the Soviet Union we have a concert again. The energies of the great powers are now once more directed not against each other, but to working out collective compromises to manage crises and the world society generally.

The present so-called Westphalian order was distilled some time after the original Westphalian settlement of 1648. That settlement established in the European system the basic principles of sovereignty, independence and equality which had been the working practice of the anti-hegemonial coalition that defeated the Habsburgs. But alongside those concepts the Westphalian settlement left in place the realistic practice of a very hierarchical ordering of the member states, with the King of France and the Holy Roman Emperor disputing the top position. Nearly all the smaller states in the Europe of 1648, mainly city states and petty princes, have disappeared. Almost all the smaller and weaker states in today's system are former European colonies, set up by Europeans as dependent states on the European model.

Decolonization and multiple independences

Decolonization was hailed by many as the world-wide fulfilment of the neo-Westphalian principles. But in fact the last phase of the proliferation of independences strained those principles to bursting point.

The European colonizers who came from the Atlantic fringe and from Russia were animated by many motives. Their main motivation was economic: they were driven by the dynamic of private enterprise, especially in their expansion eastward to "the Indies." The long range trade with Asia was a major step towards a global economy: it brought supply to meet demand at both ends of the long sea run. Transcontinental economic enterprise was profitable but dangerous. Because it was dangerous, the states which benefited from the profits and sponsored the enterprises were drawn in to protect the geese that laid the golden eggs.

In the settler colonies of the Americas, when a substantial number of settlers obtained a degree of local control and deemed themselves able to stand on their own feet, they usually seceded. Independent states were formed.

68 The future of the Westphalian anti-hegemonial system

After the Vienna settlement the collective hegemony of the Concert of Europe accepted independent settler states without difficulty as remote and neutral members of their neo-Westphalian European society. The Westphalian order was not undermined by the accession of the settler-ruled states.

The Europeans did not at first attempt to apply their Westphalian arrangements to those areas outside the European *grande république* which were for various reasons unsuitable for white settlers. But in the course of the nineteenth century they extended their neo-Westphalian principles to the whole world. Not merely the economy was becoming globalized, but the states system and the rules of international society too. The Europeans recognized all independent states as juridically equal, but assigned a dependent status to much of Asia, most of Africa and some other areas. In Asia, European trading companies, in order to make their operations safer, took on administrative functions, usually on behalf of Asian rulers. When the European-controlled areas became too large for the companies, European imperial governments rather reluctantly took over the administration, and established European-style dependent states. Each imperial government was regarded as exclusively responsible for the governance of the dependent states which it set up. It was a *cuius regio eius lex*.

Until the great technological revolution began in the West some two hundred years ago, the high Asian civilizations—China, India, Japan, Persia—seemed to thoughtful Europeans more advanced than their own. It was fashionable to admire not only "the wisdom of the East", but also the technical superiority of many of the Asian manufactures that European traders brought back. But when technological innovation put the Europeans far ahead, they came to believe that their superiority extended beyond its technological and economic context: they acquired notions of racial and cultural superiority too.

Imperial governments and publics began to develop the sense of responsibility for the well-being of non-European peoples, and the obligation to extend (European) standards of civilization to those peoples, which are such striking features of today's collective hegemony. They discharged this obligation in Asia either by colonial administration in India, Russian central Asia, Indonesia etc. or by pressure and inducement in Japan, China and Persia. The self-assumed obligation of Europeans and North Americans, to reform the internal affairs of non-European states which they recognized as independent, was parallel to the same assumption by the Concert in Europe. Both ran counter to the Westphalian tenet of non-interference. The practice of the global international system began to acquire a markedly core–periphery shape.

Meanwhile both government and business administration in the Asian dependent states was increasingly turned over to European-educated élites. Given the high levels of Asian civilizations, this reversion to Asian hands was to be expected.

The future of the Westphalian anti-hegemonial system 69

The precept of the moral obligation of highly civilized states and communities towards less civilized ones was at first ahead of the practice; but it was significant. The suppression of the slave trade (but not yet slavery) was written into the Vienna settlement of 1815. As early as 1833 a British parliamentary committee on India proclaimed "the indisputable principle that the interests of the native subjects are to be consulted in preference to those of Europeans whenever the two come in competition." From 1919 the League of Nations mandates and later the UN trusteeships marked another milestone. Individual core powers took over from their defeated enemies the responsibility for bringing this or that peripheral people to acceptable standards of civilization and to self-government; but the process was subjected to international supervision through the League or the United Nations. The colonies of the imperial powers were not legally affected; but the mandate–trustee rules influenced colonial practice. The responsibility was made more specific and partially collectivized.

The Versailles settlement also made international society, or in practice the largest member states of the League of Nations, responsible for the strategic security of the weaker members who could not provide it for themselves. Collective security was in fact a move away from doctrinal anarchy, a frail attempt to find a substitute for the maintenance of order by the Concert of Europe. In that sense it was a core–periphery formula (with a pathetically inadequate core). But it seemed Westphalian because it aimed to protect the right of all sovereign states to conduct their affairs without interference.

The great decolonization that followed World War Two began with the withdrawal of the last top layers of Western administration from Asia. The Indian sub-continent was decolonized within two years of the war's end, and almost all the rest of Asia soon after. With exceptions the newly independent Asian states were successful, and economic relations with the former imperial powers continued to flourish.

Now at the end of the twentieth century the long civilized societies of Asia have been transformed, both by technology and by contact with, and sometimes government by, Europeans and North Americans. Asia is now in the process of resuming its traditional position of technological, economic and cultural equivalence with the West.

The resurgence of Asia, and especially the inclusion of Asian powers in the Concert or core group, will affect the functioning of the emerging hegemonial international society in many ways. The cultural and administrative traditions of the great Asian civilizations—China and Japan and to a lesser extent India—are more hierarchical and suzerain than European practice since Westphalia, let alone the theory of a community composed entirely of independent and juridically equal states. The Asians, more than the Europeans, have thought in terms of imperial centres surrounded by zones of dominion and hegemonic authority. The Chinese tradition in particular includes responsibility of the Central Kingdom for its periphery, with a net outflow of material resources as well as less tangible benefits of civilization. Indians like Professor A.P. Rana are suggesting that the Concert should delegate to individual major powers the responsibility for carrying out Concert decisions in neighbouring areas. Such arrangements would make it difficult for both these great Asian powers to continue their rhetoric in favour of inviolable Westphalian sovereignty.

It is otherwise in sub-saharan Africa and Oceania, and largely (except for the European settlers) in the Caribbean. Up to about a century ago, these peoples had no such grass roots civilization as Asia had. They were like my ancestors when Julius Caesar landed in Britain—"noble savages" but pre-literate. Western education has produced able individual élites, but not communities capable of managing a modern economy and a modern state unaided. However, after World War Two the sentiment grew, not least in imperial countries like Britain and France, that colonial rule by a single power, whether beneficial to the governed or not, was now an anachronism and ought to be ended.

Wholesale decolonization was inevitable when it became clear to business enterprises and to governments in the imperial countries that it would pay to yield to the demands of the Western-educated élites to take over the dependent states—as some said, to step into the colonizers' shoes—and also to the pressure of both superpowers. So almost all the dependent states—colonies, mandates, protectorates, Soviet Republics—were accorded nominal independence. The number of members of the United Nations has risen to three times what it was originally. Independence has become a status or rank, and indeed the only acceptable one. But that does not mean that the new states are able to stand on their own feet, as earlier decolonized states were obliged to do. Webster's dictionary gives three conditions of independence: freedom from outside control; (financial) self-sufficiency; and direction of one's affairs without interference. It is unreasonable to expect the great majority of newly decolonized states outside Asia to achieve these conditions soon.

Until the wholesale grant of independence to incompetent states began in earnest in the 1960s, it was plausible to regard the international society as essentially neo-Westphalian. It was possible to consider the non-Westphalian features of the Cold War period, like the hegemony and the core–periphery structure of both the Western and communist camps, as exceptions or aberrations. Hedley Bull's classic *The Anarchical Society*, which he compiled in the early 1970s, described the world society of states in those terms. But the hegemonial nature of the system bothered him, because it does not fit Westphalian principles. *The Anarchical Society* avoids the subject; but he encouraged me to write an analysis of hegemony.

In practice the Western powers, when engaged in their struggle with the communist world, found on their hands a large periphery that was incapable of managing economically. They realized that an anarchical society extended in this impractical way would not function by itself, or even with occasional

The future of the Westphalian anti-hegemonial system 71

and exceptional help to its weakest members. Some general substitiute was needed for the underpinning which colonial authority had provided. The Western powers therefore developed a complex and patchy but fairly inclusive pattern of collective economic security for non-communist peripheral states. Much of the necessary aid to each ex-colony continued to be supplied by the former imperial power. The collapse of the Soviet Union has ended the danger to the West of Soviet influence in the "third world." But that has not stopped the core of developed states—the present concert of donors—from accepting responsibility for the periphery. The donors in fact continue to extend the mutually beneficial arrangements for collective economic support. Robert Jackson has pointed out that more than half the states in the periphery are now both defended and paid for by the core states. Kofi Annan, the realistic Secretary-General of the United Nations, recently told his fellow Africans to stop blaming colonialism for the woes of the continent, and to set out on the long and difficult path to higher standards, with the help of what the outline above calls the postmodern states at the core.

The Western donor powers are not finding it easy to establish their standards of civilization—human rights, social justice, democracy, protection of the environment etc.—in return for their aid. The failed states and ministates can label themselves democracies, but they cannot achieve Western standards. The concept of independence for all political entities that want it is an idea that the élites learnt from the West. It was fine in the struggle to throw off European dominance. But the élites have found how shaky their newly-acquired authority is in the Western-type states bequeathed them by the Europeans. In some African states order has collapsed. The élites have become acutely aware of the need for strong government, and of the danger to order and to their personal positions posed by destabilizing Western ideas on individual human rights. The rulers of the decolonized former SSRs of the Russian empire are in the same position: their governments are much more authoritarian than that of Russia. In general most peripheral governments will continue for some time to feel a need for firm control to maintain order and suppress opposition. They will therefore want to retain as much of their Westphalian sovereignty as the Western concert powers will let them.

The core and the periphery

The core–periphery order has taken a long time to evolve. The political and administrative leaders who shaped the policies of the great powers did not implement a theoretical plan for it, or foresee very clearly how it would develop. They worked out ad hoc responses to the pressures of the globalizing system. Their expedients developed into tacitly accepted codes of conduct, and sometimes solidified into institutions. In a sense the global expansion of the rules and standards of the European international society to cover the whole world was an earlier core–periphery experiment. The same is true of the entire colonial experience outside the European settler

72 The future of the Westphalian anti-hegemonial system

areas: especially the collective aspects of the mandate and trusteeship regimes and the concerted interventions in China, which remained technically an independent state. Contemporary instruments of collective hegemony like the International Monetary Fund are developing their functions in the same experimental way.

Though we are still in the experimental stage today, the pattern is becoming much clearer now. We see long term trends gathering momentum and interacting with each other to erode the rules and principles of the Westphalian order. Decolonization might seem a triumph of Westphalian principles; but by creating so many nominally independent but unviable states, it has strengthened rather than diminished the development of a core–periphery order. The resurgence of Asia has produced some Westphalian rhetoric about non-interference in the internal affairs of states; but the great powers of Asia are likely to work for the delegation to them of hegemonial responsibilities for administering, in their own peripheries, the compromise decisions reached by the collective core. The growing Western sense of responsibility, especially in the United States, for how other countries run their internal affairs may be the most important force for change of all. Hegemonial pressure by the core states has become increasingly collectivized. It has produced a whole codex of international treaties and agreements on human rights and the environment; and the agreements legitimize further hegemonial pressure and intervention. These three trends, acting within the inexorable net of tightening global interdependence, have helped to sweep away the anarchophile and anti-hegemonial spirit of the Westphalian order that was designed for Europe. But the neo-Westphalian rules and quasi-Westphalian institutions like the United Nations still remain largely in place.

A great power is not a legal status but a fact. At present the great powers consist of the five permanent members of the Security Council (the United States, China, France, Britain and Russia) plus the other members of the Group of Seven/Eight (Japan, Germany, Italy and Canada). With them are associated other minor donor powers. We may expect the whole European Union to act more as one in relation to the periphery. These powers exercise a collective hegemonial authority which continues to grow. The hegemony of the core concert corresponds to the dependence of the peripheral recipients, and is made a practising reality by that dependence. Indeed many operations of the present collective hegemony are called into being by the inadequacy of the majority of the nominally independent states in the system, and the obligation felt by the donor powers both to respond to the demands of the recipients and at the same time to lay down the conditions for giving aid.

We can range the two-hundred or so independent states in the present international society in a recipient–donor list, according to how much help they get or give. At the top we will find some fifty obscure small states quite unable to manage by themselves, and at the bottom some twenty rich powerful donors led by Japan, United States and Western Europe, supporting the whole core–periphery structure on their shoulders like Atlas. One interesting thing about this list is its durability. A similar list drawn up fourscore years ago, say in 1920, would range the political entities in much the same order, though two thirds of the states in the list were then formally classed as dependencies.

Intervention in the internal affairs of nominally independent recipients of aid, and of other peripheral states also, is now taken for granted. Indeed not to intervene is widely regarded, both by Western public opinion and by sufferers in the periphery, as a failure by the great powers to meet their international responsibilities. The President of the United States recently apologized publicly for not intervening to stop the genocide in Rwanda. (The responsibility of great powers is a very old idea. In one of the most striking passages in Thucydides, the envoys from Corinth tell their great Spartan allies that "the true author of the subjugation of a polis is not so much the immediate agent as the power which permits it though it could prevent it." Ole Wæver calls the contemporary form of hegemonial responsibility "neo-Sumerian.")

Some Western concert powers discharge what they see as their obligations to the dependent periphery with increasing reluctance. There is much evidence of public donor fatigue over aid involving taxpayers' money. And the reluctance to shed their blood in military operations to promote good causes is even more marked. We must not therefore assume that the donors at the core of international society will continue to increase the scope of their interventions. The long term supertanker of the responsibility of the core for the periphery may perhaps be slowing down. What does seem likely is that the donors will raise the price in acceptable behaviour which they demand in return for their aid.

The determining nexus of a core–periphery system is not relations with the periphery but the relations between the core powers. We may be able to gain some idea of how the international system will function in the near future if we look at the practice of concerts, including the present one. A collective hegemony or concert is a continuous ongoing relationship. Its members are normally involved with each other over a number of problems at once. The problems are usually complex, and occur in different parts of the system. In recent months a coordinated effort by the world economic concert has provided massive financial support on an unprecedented scale to a number of states in East Asia, with far-reaching conditions. It is negotiated and administered by the International Monetary Fund acting on behalf of the major economic powers who subscribed the money. The concert uses different but concerted methods to cope with the intractable problems of weapons of mass destruction in Iraq and North Korea, and in India and Pakistan. In the Korean case we see four-state negotiations strikingly co-chaired by the United States and China. The concert is using other arrangements, including intervention by NATO, to mitigate internal disorder: fairly effectively in the former Yugoslavia but less successfully and less willingly in several African states.

Each future problem will concern some concert powers more than others; but in their discussions there is always a certain linkage, even a trade-off, between the various problems. One advantage of a collective over a single hegemony is that its policies are compromises that result from checks and balances within the concert, and a concert is elastic enough to let its members sometimes play different roles. Concert powers have often disagreed in the past, and will do so in the future; and nowadays the media play up these disagreements. The operation of a collective hegemony does not require all the concert powers to agree with and endorse every hegemonial action or pressure, let alone actively participate in every action. It does involve prior discussion, and then acquiescence by the dissenting concert powers, though sometimes reluctantly and under protest (as China has acquiesced and withheld its veto dozens of times in the Security Council of the United Nations). And because the powers will need to concert action in many fields for the foreseeable future, the powers that decide to take an action not endorsed by all of them will be careful to tailor that action to take account of the objections of the doubters, so that even the most apparently unilateral actions involve more compromise and more *raison de système* than appears on the surface, in order to make the collective hegemony work. As Asian powers acquire stronger positions in the concert, the pressures for compromise will grow.

The tendency of a concert relationship to pull the policies of its members into alignment with each other presents difficulties for democracies, especially those whose national mythology glorifies independence and whose publics think in neo-Westphalian terms. Most of all this is true of the United States. Democratic governments therefore tend to present their external actions to their publics as more independent and more based on moral principles than in fact they are; and discussion in legislatures and the media widens the gap between reality and justification. The nature of the core–periphery order is therefore less visible than it might be.

The core and the periphery: transfer of resources

The distribution of resources from donors to recipients is now only partially from a donor state or institution representing donor states to a recipient state. In our present phase rich and powerful states assume some burdens and provide some resources to weaker and less developed states; burdens which those weaker states would have to assume for themselves under a stricter definition of independence. An obvious burden is the general provision of defence against aggression. Outside inter-state relations and in parallel to them, in recent decades we have seen a growing multi-channel transfer of private resources, especially investment and know-how, outward from the rich centre to the less rich periphery. The volume of these private resources considerably exceeds the investment by the imperial powers before decolonization. States play only a limited part in this great centrifuge. Resources are usually transferred when they generate more profit in the periphery than the core.

We are no longer so bewitched as we were by Marxist theory and other ideas about state-controlled economies. The gradual integration of the world into a single economy can now be seen as the spinning of a vast web of private enterprise, with states trying to protect and regulate it. The aim of private enterprise is to supply consumer demand as profitably as possible. From the cannon and the compass of the early sailing ships through the industrial revolution to the rapid development of modern technology, the innovations which private enterprise generates are making the global integration of the economy ever more feasible and ever more a reality. As techniques of manufacturing, financial services and marketing become ever more sophisticated, competitive private enterprise is becoming steadily more effective than cumbersome state bureaucracy at producing wealth.

Some far ranging enterprises are detaching themselves from a particular state, and becoming pipelines connecting sources of production and consumption round the world. In particular the relentless (and surely very desirable) rise in the remuneration of labour relative to other costs has now reached between two thirds and three quarters of all costs in the core economies. Such companies will therefore continue to move labour-intensive operations to the periphery. Each shift involves the transfer of the necessary capital investment, technical know-how and, equally important, guaranteed markets in core economies. (Costa Rica is a good example. Its principal exports used to be coffee and bananas. Now first place has been taken by a range of products each of which is a stage in a manufacturing process, from microchips to textiles, with labour paid sometimes double the local rates. This involvement of the periphery in core industry enriches both the Costa Rican economy and the companies.) The "offshore" arrangements of private companies establish durable patterns of mutual involvement that affect jobs, prices, infrastructure and ultimately votes in both the core and the periphery. The entanglement of the more and less developed economies is becoming more institutionalized and more permanent. This may well be the pattern of the future.

The concert of donor states used to be perceived as operating in a neo-Westphalian inter-state system: offering aid, and laying down conditions for that aid, across the frontiers of what were nevertheless "independent" states. But the system is now becoming ever more visibly supra-national. The operations of the concert governments are designed primarily to ensure the increasing production of wealth by private enterprise, both for the donors (of course) and also for the recipients. The concert in its present phase of Western and particularly US dominance, is also concerned to promote Western standards of civilization and human rights in the periphery, and to protect the environment, largely from the ruthlessness of some private enterprises.

76 The future of the Westphalian anti-hegemonial system

In order to achieve these ends in a more institutionalized future hegemony, the concert powers will want to ensure the following conditions:

1) Peace between states, that is, the suppression of military inter-state conflict.
2) The supression of armed conflicts between factions inside states: in other words the maintenance of domestic order.
3) The enforcement (by local states if possible, but where necessary under pressure or even intervention by the concert) of commercial property and other laws, and banking and other competitive practices, that are designed to make outside investment and the production of wealth safer.
4) The concert, and especially its Western members, will doubtless continue to exert substantial pressure on most of the recipient states in order to induce them to foster the standards of civilization (human rights, democracy, the environment etc.) which the West wishes to see.

Recipient states, which make up most of the very diverse periphery, are anxious to receive the investment, know-how and access to markets which core states and private corporations are willing to offer. They will probably become increasingly ready to accept the conditions that the core states attach, including the adoption of Western standards of civilization. Interdependence seems likely to become more acceptable in the peripheral world. The pressures of technology are inescapable. Moreover the populations of the peripheral world have rising expectations of material benefits, and they welcome the material advantages which integration brings to them. The benefits diminish social unrest, and so also make the positions of the ruling élites more secure.

Our understanding of the hegemonial concert requires us to recognize that there is at present no other effective force in favour of the mundane aims listed above. Let us imagine that some colossal upsurge of donor fatigue, moral indifference and economic protectionism removed all hegemonial pressures, inducements and aid from the international scene. Who will doubt that economic prosperity, human rights and even international peace and order would sharply decline?

Butterfield and Wight stated in a well-known phrase that the (Westphalian) states system is held together by prudence and moral obligation. The two principles usually point in the same direction: but not always. In the dealings of the core with the periphery there are possible conflicts. Prudence will in future form ties and produces rules designed to mitigate friction and loss and to produce material advantages to both sides, sometimes at the expense of moral values; whereas the commitments of moral responsibility may involve material costs. In the compromises hammered out between the great powers, and between them and the periphery, prudent and mundane advantages are likely to have a more general appeal than controversial moral values. Therefore prudence is likely to prevail.

If the situation remains reasonably benign, the collective hegemony may be able to achieve its mundane and material aims. However, specific events are unpredictable. There have been civil wars in both China and Russia in the twentieth century: further chaos is a possibility in either great country. Might an anti-hegemonial split in the concert divide the world into two opposing camps again? Could there be another economic slump on the scale of 1929? What may happen in Islam, the huge area from Morocco to Indonesia, from Kazakhstan to Cameroon? How great is the danger from nuclear and other weapons of mass destruction? A disaster arising in one of these contexts, or a quite unforeseen one, could cause another abrupt discontinuity in the international system. Long term trends would be forced to take other forms.

But if events do stay benign, it is possible to picture the hegemonial core concert establishing itself as a supranational authority. It would gain legitimacy partly by leaving a place for limited national independences; and partly also by developing programmes that appeal to the majority of people throughout the world, and ensuring that these programmes are put into force both at home and in the periphery. Such policies would have to be less exclusively Western. There is much evidence that the concert's present policies respond to the widespread desire for peace and order, for higher standards of living, and some human rights. So long as the pendulum keeps swinging in its present direction, the concert of great powers, and especially the United States, are capable of becoming increasingly the joint trustees and executors of a general will of mankind.

The decline of the sovereign state?

This paper is not intended to discuss the role of the state as such. I do not think it is reasonable to fear, as some claim, that economic liberalization is hollowing-out all states, and the multinational agencies that serve them, so that they will become mere shells. Even if states abandon all efforts to own and operate sectors of the economy, on a wider perspective the role of governments in modern public life seems certain to continue in a great range from order, justice and legislation through activities like education and defence to the regulation of private enterprise. In the Western core, economic liberalization or privatization is a policy carried out by states, and states also dictate the present policy of the international agencies to encourage private rather than state enterprise in the periphery. The carrots and sticks of the donor powers and their agencies are directed at recipient states, to induce those states to deregulate and internationalize their economies and to conform to Western standards.

The question at issue here is the more limited one of whether, as a matter of principle and law, governmental authority will continue to be vested exclusively or almost exclusively in territorially delimited sovereign states. Here the answer seems to be: in practice no. We seem to be moving towards greater surrender of powers by individual states to supranational bodies and regional organizations in various specific fields like arms control, the environment and finance. These organizations will be controlled, and their powers reinforced, by the hegemonial authority of the core, much as for instance the International Monetary Fund is controlled today. The bundle that we used to call sovereignty is being undone into separate pieces. Moreover the practice of the system has moved, and is still moving, so far from the Westphalian concept that the rules are likely to alter also, in order to correspond to changing practice.

The European Union is a special case. If the member states merge into a confederacy, and turn over powers like external relations and defence as well as economic policy to confederal authorities, then the European Union may well become a federal state, and will take its place in the concert alongside other federal states. But is it possible that Europe will develop a new form of government, something more closely integrated than a league (Staatenbund) and less integrated than a federal state (Bundesstaat)—something perhaps like the Holy Roman Empire? None of these interesting special forms will radically affect the general nature of the system, or the evolution from a Westphalian to a core–periphery order.

The world continues to shrink. The tightening net of technology and global integration, as well as the core–periphery structure of the international system, are bound to reduce the "independence" of all states, including the largest and most powerful. In addition the global pressures will limit the weaker states of the periphery, especially the ministates and failed states, to a smaller scope of jurisdiction which might be called sovereign autonomy. Many nation-states will, I believe, find their newly-acquired sovereignty increasingly limited, so that they will tend to become in practice more like autonomous provinces of an increasingly integrated world system. But they will not disappear. Their function will be local administration and regulation. A few may operate under collective policing or occupation: we will doubtless see more Haitis and Bosnias. The rest will provide increasing social services on lines demanded by their publics and the donor powers, and with resources substantially generated in one way or another by donor investment and other forms of aid.

But this small residue of sovereignty is likely to retain the Westphalian symbols of independence—the flag, the embassies, the seat at the United Nations—and the right to refuse hegemonial demands and conditions (the ability to do so in practice is another matter). A maxim of European statecraft says that if you want to change the wine, don't change the label on the bottle.

Summing up

In sum, and leaving the unforeseeable aside, what can we expect the characteristics of the "international" system to look like in the near future? No answer can be more than an informed guess. Here are my guesses:

The future of the Westphalian anti-hegemonial system

- Economic globalization will gradually erode the Westphalian concept of independent territorial states. But this process will encounter nationalist, protectionist and anti-hegemonial resistance.
- The legitimacy, the laws and institutions of the global international society are largely Westphalian. But Westphalian legitimacy will not prevent the further development in practice of a hegemonial core–periphery pattern which has been taking shape for a long time.
- The granting of nominal independence to almost every political entity that wanted it seemed the ultimate extension of anarchic Westphalianism. But the continuing dependence on outside help of many failed or inadequate states will make the core–periphery nature of the society increasingly obvious.
- The Westphalian ban on interference in the internal affairs of states is now virtually in abeyance and may soon formally collapse.
- The informal concert of great powers, which forms the single core of the present system, has operated only since the collapse of the Soviet Union. It may come to function more smoothly, and perhaps become more institutionalized into an overarching supranational authority. Asian powers will come to play a greater role.
- The concert will be less concerned with maintaining a system of separate states, and concentrate more on a quest for peace and prosperity: that is, on avoiding armed conflict and creating conditions for increasing material wealth. It will rely more on private enterprise to produce the wealth. But the Western components of the core will look to peripheral governments where possible to enforce locally the standards of civilization (human rights and social justice, the protection of the environment, etc.) prescribed by the core.
- The policies of the concert will thus further break down the barriers which still separate states from each other. Both globlization of the world economy (which is not primarily a function of states) and pressure for Western standards of civilization (which is such a function) will continue to integrate the world system.

However, Westphalian states will not soon outwardly disappear. Much of the facade of the present society will continue to survive, just as its formal aspects survived earlier breaches of its practice. The real independence of states will continue to erode; but states, large and small, will retain the outward forms of independence and some real internal autonomy.

10 International relations and the practice of hegemony

I want to offer you some thoughts about how relations across state boundaries tend to function in times of hegemony.

Definitions of hegemony

Let me specify what I mean by hegemony. In discussions of international relations theory it tends to have two meanings. One has to do with the distribution of power in a system. Not merely military force, but also technical and financial strength. The other meaning is the dominance of a particular idea or set of assumptions, such as economic liberalism and globalization.

I certainly use the term hegemony primarily in the first sense. It is the material condition that enables one great power, or a group of powers, or the great powers in a system acting collectively, to bring such great pressures and inducements to bear that most other states lose some of their freedom of action de facto, though not de iure.

I formerly thought of hegemony as that area of the spectrum between multiple absolute independences and a single world government that allows dominant powers to influence the external policies of other states, but not or only marginally their domestic policies. Now I realize how much the hegemony of the West and especially the United States also aims to modify the internal behaviour of other states and communities.

So of course ideas also play their part—especially the ideas of the hegemonic communities. At present these ideas certainly include economic liberalism, the belief in the greater relative effectiveness of private enterprise; and globalization. But that is much too limited a list. Equally prominent today are Western standards of civilization, human rights and the environment. And I think we must include a heightened awareness of the moral responsibilities that go with power, however much these responsibilities are shirked.

This concept of a hegemonic system refers in the first place to dealings between governments. But not merely that. I want also to look at an area that is becoming very crowded with comment, namely the activities of the many different kinds of non-governmental organizations (NGOs), and the pressures which they exert both on governments and directly across state boundaries. This is the grey area between the concept of a state-centred, state-dominated international society and a world of many interests and pressure groups, a so-called world society in which even hegemonial governments may be as much pressurized as pressurizing.

Rosenau summed it up in 1990 with his formula: "The state-centric system now coexists with an equally powerful, though more decentralized, multi-centric system."

The search of the British Committee for an international theory had to begin at the beginning. It was at first concentrated on the relations between states, and indeed between the executive branches of governments, often even limited to independent governments. The states system was compared to the solar system, where planets and moons are very separate self-contained entities which nonetheless influence each other.

This concentration on relations between independent states is part of what Buzan and Little call the Westphalian straitjacket, and I think also the Westphalian ghetto.

We are now aware that the early concentration of international relations theory on systems of independent states prevented us from dealing systematically enough with hegemonic and suzerain systems. If Martin Wight was right in calling the European system "a succession of hegemonies"—as I believe he was—we need to examine the operational practice of each hegemony or bid for hegemony in all its individuality, and then compare them with each other and with the present phase of hegemony. Here we have not done our homework. My book *The Evolution of International Society* is only a start.

Similarly we also need to study more systematically the impact of non-governmental actors on international systems. These are not separate subjects. I hope to indicate the connection between the two.

The world of states

To take the world of states first. No system of states can function without some rules and understandings about how its members conduct their dealings. In the international society defined by Hedley Bull in his classic *The Anarchical Society*, member states, especially the big ones, consciously put in place, and continually modify, elaborate rules and institutions to manage their relations. Diplomacy and war are part of the dialogue between states.

And in all these activities the power of the largest states tells. So that even in Westphalian systems we see a glimmer of that great power governance, and sometimes the pre-eminence of one superpower, that we associate with hegemony.

Superior power is due to technology. In the modern world technology radiates outwards from the areas where it is generated. Perhaps this was always so, as Professor MacNeill and others say. And moral values, standards of civilization, expand on the back of the technology.

I have also become increasingly aware of the underlying continuities along the spectrum. We tend to pay too much attention to differences. We think too much in terms of either/or. And we tend to forget that not every part of a complex international system is at the same point along the spectrum at any one time.

Climate of ideas

We are now living in a period when the pendulum is visibly moving along the spectrum, away from multiple independences into the area of hegemony. When this happens some tendencies, some ways of thinking and behaving that we associate with Westphalian systems, decline, while others that we associate with hegemony wax stronger.

When we talk of times of hegemony, we refer to what actually occurs in the international field, and also to what people think ought to occur. A useful indication of the shift in the climate of opinion from Westphalian independence to hegemonial constraint is the buzz words which help to formulate in our minds the patterns of international reality.

Ideas like:

- sovereignty
- anti-hegemonial coalitions
- balance of power (especially)
- juridical equality of states
- non-intervention
- splendid isolation
- the Republican party's aim of aloofness in the United States today

come from the multiple independences end of the spectrum.

But ideas like:

- management of the international system
- privileges and responsibilities of great powers and rich nations
- Concert of Europe
- intervention
- standards of civilization
- human rights and women's rights
- donor and recipient states
- strings to aid
- derogations of sovereignty
- limits to independence

come from the hegemony–suzerainty area of the spectrum.

Intervention designed to change the *internal* conduct of another, weaker state, is an un-Westphalian concept. It is a hegemonial act. Today we have not merely occasional interventions to correct a specific imbalance or right a specific injustice. We have sustained aid and interventionist pressure, on what is in practice a permanent basis. And where we don't intervene, there is a feeling that we ought to. Think of the President of the United States publicly apologizing to Rwanda after the massacre of 500,000 people there, for not intervening to stop it.

Three tendencies in the policies of great powers, the governments of developed states, help to shape the international system:

1) National interest or Imperialism.
2) Prudence: which means minimizing risks to the state itself and also to the international society in which it operates. It involves seeking the agreement, or at least the acquiescence, of the other great powers most concerned.
3) Moral responsibility.

All three of these tendencies are normally present together in the policies of major developed powers. Both in Westphalian and hegemonic times. I would like to offer you an illustration of how these three tendencies can work in practice, from a previous hegemonic period: namely, the collective resolution by the great powers of the Eastern Crisis of 1878. I can do so later if people are interested.

Professor Inis Claude, who has given much thought to the activities of developed states in times of hegemony, wrote to me on 29 November 2001.

> There are ... many inadequately explored issues relating to hegemonial responsibilities for dealing with the inadequacies, injustices and instabilities that are rampant in today's world.
>
> On thinking about the erosion of sovereignty and the state itself brought about by collective hegemony and its interventionist practice, I raise the issue as to whether such external interference may not have the opposite effect. Indeed, most of our interventions have the ostensible purpose—if not always the actual result—of making the target state *more* capable and more effective (as well as more acceptable) in meeting the needs of its society. Is collective state-diminution offset by collective state-building, state-improving, state-stabilization etc?

I agree with Inis Claude that in general the effect of hegemonial aid and intervention is to make weak states more effective: that is, more capable of carrying out the policies agreed with the donors and interveners. These policies are largely determined outside the recipient state. They involve measures specified by the donors and enforcers, but carried out by the government of the recipient state. But not only that. They usually also include the creation of conditions in which non-state actors based outside the recipient state, from banks and businesses to doctors and human rights advocates, can operate more safely and more effectively.

In other words, I think there is a rule of thumb here. At least in the medium term, hegemonial inducements and pressures make recipient states more efficient but less independent.

In the hegemonial range of the spectrum, the purposes of the donor and interventionist states are achieved largely by *proxy*. Especially when the swing of the pendulum is away from a Westphalian system towards greater hegemony, the recipient states retain the trappings of independent sovereignty: the flags, the embassies, the seats at the United Nations. Also some interventions, whether unilateral or by multilateral agencies, have the ostensible Westphalian purpose of making the recipient state outgrow its dependence and become as truly independent as a small weak state can aspire to be. This is what Claude calls "post-independence trusteeship." It is particularly true of the rhetoric of US aid and intervention, and I believe its long term intention. The US government and public opinion see their international aims in Westphalian terms.

These trappings of nominal independence and equality help to make hegemonial authority more palatable in recipient states. They lend *legitimacy* to hegemonial practice. And legitimacy is the lubricating oil of international relations.

When we look at these shifts within the pattern, we can see that one of the forces that has moved the pendulum back in our lifetimes from Westphalian independence towards hegemonial aid and intervention is the fact that, while some of the dependent states have succeeded in managing their newly won independence in the modern world, all too many have not been able to do so on their own. These failures disturb both governments and public opinion in developed states.

In this context there has been some discussion of whether the key factor in the operation of hegemonies is that the strongest powers seek to impose stability on the periphery. Some members of the realist school have developed a hegemonic stability theory. This is often too narrow. Today's hegemonic Western great powers conspicuously seek not merely stability, not merely law and order, but also democracy, human rights, and the rest of the Western standards.

It is a dilemma of Western powers that in many recipient states these objectives conflict. When they do, Western governments tend to give priority to stability. For stability, in addition to its own merits, is arguably a prerequisite of prosperity, human rights, and other values. But not all morally animated NGOs accept this argument. Some are still committed to anarchophilia.

If we look further along the spectrum, towards more imperial systems, we see increasingly firm and prolonged intervention and diminishing de iure independence. The implementation of the policies of the hegemonial powers by the governments of autonomous states gives way to more efficient and more direct administration of dependent states that implement the policies of a single imperial power. This is what is loosely called colonialism. Or a group of great powers may install a collective dependent state, as for instance in Bosnia.

When we look in the other direction, back towards the Westphalian area of the spectrum, we see aid and intervention decrease. Weak states become more sovereign, and often less effective. The hypothetical end-system of absolute de facto as well as de iure independences has never existed in practice. At that extreme point no government would feel moral responsibility for what might happen outside its own borders, and be motivated only by *raison d'état*.

This business of looking both ways, like the Russian imperial eagle, is very significant for our understanding of the characteristics of hegemonial systems. It enables us to see (what Claude calls) hegemonial state-building and state-improvement in the periphery of the system as a half-way house between on the one hand the colonial practice of building stable and effective but dependent states, and on the other hand the Westphalian granting of independence to all dependent states. In almost every case, they are the same states, in the same borders. It is the degree of dependence which changes.

What about managing the system itself? As the pendulum swings towards hegemony, we can see how system management expands from the limited Westphalian practice—that is, collective management by states of the impersonal pressures of their mutual involvement—into the present hegemonic practice of world-wide propagation of what Bull and I called "Western values" and what Vincent called the "diplomacy of justice."

These are mutations, but mutations of the same underlying pattern.

Non-governmental organizations

Now for the non-governmental side of the picture.

NGOs is a vast catch-all term. We are concerned here with transnational organizations: that is, those which influence or try to influence the situation in countries other than their own.

Generalizations are difficult, as one would expect with such a large and varied group. I think that on balance it is better to treat all non-governmental actors as a single range, and to look at their similarities as well as their differences. But some scholars consider that they get a clearer picture of how the present international system, and especially the concept of a global civil society, function if economic enterprises are treated separately from ethically motivated NGOs. Perhaps we need both approaches.

The most important and powerful category of transnational NGOs is economic interests of every kind. It includes not only corporations and banks etc. but also trade unions and consumers. Transnational businesses aim to make money by supplying goods or services that their customers in various states want. They become involved in our equation because they have to operate in ways acceptable to the governments of foreign states as well as their own. Transnational businesses bring pressures and inducements to bear on all the governments they have to deal with and vice versa. The most interesting businesses in this category are those which have become effectively detached from any one state, and make a profit or fee by bringing supply to meet demand world-wide.

Enterprises within a given industry will collaborate to bring pressure on a government, while competing among themselves. So, too, trade unions compete with business managements on their members' share of the profits, but work with them to bring pressures on governments. And governments always have in mind that economic enterprises, both domestic and foreign, produce tax revenue. I will come back to this web of relationships in a moment.

Economic enterprises usually conduct their relations with governments quietly, avoiding publicity. That is in contrast to another range of NGOs, consisting of organized pressure groups with moral causes, that channel selective public indignation onto governments. These special interest groups range from religious and ideological bodies through all sorts of well-intentioned concerns. Many rely on attracting public support through the media by agitation and propaganda.

A third, smaller but interesting category of philanthropic enterprises are organized to operate not for profit but for ethical reasons. They work in areas like agriculture, medicine and education, directly in backward countries and in communities whose values are different from those of the West.

Virtually all members of these categories want to induce Western governments to promote their cause by wielding hegemonial carrots and sticks in underdeveloped states.

There is a rapidly growing academic interest in the international role of NGOs in times of hegemony. This is for the pertinent reason that hegemony seems to be the area of the spectrum that brings non-state actors most into play across state borders.

In times of multiple independences even the more powerful governments interfere in the internal affairs of other sovereign states only where it is in their state interest, including of course the state's economic interest. And the citizens of Westphalian states largely hold the same view. They may remonstrate; but they do not expect their state to intervene for moral reasons.

The economic reach of a community—the area of trade—normally stretches far beyond the area of administration. When an area of the trade partnership becomes so chaotic as to make trade difficult, the economic NGOs of a powerful state might induce that state to intervene in the national interest. It is not that trade follows the flag. More usually the flag—the gunboat diplomacy—follows trade.

On the other side of hegemony, in the area of dominion and colonization (which usually does not cover the whole system), governments come under greater pressure from NGOs, both economic and ethical. On the whole Western imperial governments have wanted above all law and order in their dependent states; and in this they have had the support of economic enterprises in the area. But law and order also requires the acquiescence of the governed. So in their own dependencies Western governments enforced what they considered to be economically profitable and morally right only so far as that enforcement did not cost them the acquiescence of the governed. Here one must remember that twentieth-century colonialism was directed, in theory and largely in practice, towards full self-government for colonies, either as separate states or incorporated into the imperial power. Colonial administrations that believed they were making orderly progress towards full self-government resented what they considered to be the excessive greed of some businesses and the ill-informed and disruptive agitation and propaganda by some moral NGOs.

After World War Two the main demand of concerned NGOs was to speed up the promised independence or at least full assimilation, and to end colonial rule. In this Westphalian demand they were supported by many non-colonial governments and also, for very different reasons, by the two superpowers, the Soviet Union and the United States.

But in times of hegemony—in conditions such as the present—small and weak states find themselves somewhere on the long road between colonial administration and real as opposed to nominal Westphalian sovereignty. Most of them find that they cannot travel that road alone. Their disappointed well-wishers in the West, including the moral pressure groups, now change their principal demand. They continue to advocate democracy, human rights, the environment and other values—values which I share. But instead of Westphalian non-interference, NGOs of all kinds now urge Western governments and international bodies to lend a helping and sometimes restraining hand. Western governments sense both a national interest and a moral responsibility to act; and they have the material capacity to do so. That is why we find that powerful hegemonial carrots and sticks become common and often continuous.

And what if real and total independence turns out to be a crock of fairy gold at the end of the Westphalian rainbow, and the long road leads in fact to a world society in which states have even less sovereignty than in Europe today?

All in all, therefore, I think that NGOs seem to have the greatest international effect in hegemonial conditions like the present. They achieve this effect by bringing pressure mainly on hegemonial and potentially hegemonial governments at a time when these governments are more willing to listen and act. And NGOs also, to a lesser extent, bring pressures to bear directly on peripheral societies.

NGOs in democracies

Economic concerns bring their discreet pressures to bear on less democratic governments as well as more democratic ones. But obviously, the more democratic a state is, the more responsive its government is to public opinion, and to organizations that reflect and mobilize various segments of public opinion. It is therefore easier for ethical NGOs to mobilize public indignation in democracies.

Members of elected legislatures, especially those that are separate from the executive government, as for instance in the United States, are more sensitive to organized public pressures than professional diplomats and chiefs of staff. So they become focal points for NGOs bringing pressures to bear on government practitioners. As a striking example, the US Congress insists on every US embassy reporting every year on the human rights record of the state where the embassy is situated, and then publishing these reports. Such behaviour dismays the permanent professionals inside governments and intergovernmental bodies—the mandarins and sherpas—who try to safeguard what they see as the long term interests of their state or organization, and also to preserve a just balance between several desirable goals for the world.

The pattern of non-governmental pressure on governments repeats itself. Just as economic enterprises affect tax revenues, so ethical organizations affect votes. Both are of great concern to democratic governments.

The pattern repeats itself also in that, like transnational economic enterprises, many of the organizations that apply ethical pressure on governments are also not confined within the nutshell of one state, operating on only one government. Obvious examples are religious organizations, the Red Cross, Médecins Sans Frontières. They also interact with intergovernmental organizations like the World Bank whose interests are not circumscribed by any one state. In this period of hegemony ethical as well as commercial NGOs are becoming increasingly globalized.

So we see that in times of hegemony a great range of NGOs finds it unusually rewarding to pressurize governments of developed states, in order to change the domestic practices of other states.

What about the position in the recipient states? The governments of incompetent and failed states are usually made up of Westernized or Russianized élites. They cherish their recently won nominal independence. But they know that they cannot manage alone. They see their states, with some justification, as poor countries exploited by rich ones. And they are more keenly aware than their Western critics that full Western freedoms would make their states ungovernable—that the alternatives in their states are firm government or chaos.

Therefore these élite governments—where there is effective government as opposed to chaos—have two basic aims in their dealings with the developed world:

1. to obtain the maximum of aid—economic, access to markets, medical, and of course arms to maintain order; and also to ensure that the aid is chanelled as far as possible through their government and dispensed to the people by it. This outside aid is a major ingredient of what keeps

their government popular, or at least secures the reluctant consent of the governed.
2. to comply with what they call the neo-colonial demands of donor governments and NGOs about Western standards of civilization only so far as necessary to ensure the flow of aid.

Some recipient governments are more willing than others to collaborate with governments and NGOs of the developed West, and more skilful at doing so. Such partnerships, though unequal, can be very beneficial to the recipient community. Recipient governments can count on the vocal support of moral NGOs in donor states in their quest for material advantages. But they usually find themselves up against the same NGOs over compliance with what we can broadly call Western standards of civilization and human rights.

Of course where a less developed government has a strategic asset like a lot of oil or an indispensable base, it can afford to defy the NGOs of donor states. But otherwise, to defy these NGOs is to renounce Western aid.

Public opinion in recipient countries is hard to measure. In some there hardly is yet such a thing as a majority opinion. In my experience, most of the governed want what they conceive to be Western standards of living and of civilization more than their rulers want these things for them. But they are not effectively organized in moral NGOs.

Reverse pressures

The pressures in the NGO world are not all one way. You have reverse pressures on NGOs by both donor and recipient governments, and by intergovernmental institutions. These counter-pressures on NGOs are less than the pressures of NGOs on governments; but they are considerable.

On the economic side, you cannot draw a hard line between governments and capitalist private enterprises. There are degrees of partnership. Examples are: the East India Companies; German industry after 1871; and the industrial–military complex in the United States.

In quasi-Westphalian times a donor government cannot control what a recipient does with the aid it receives. Even in a hegemonial climate it is not easy. As well as incompetence and embezzlement, many recipient governments use their increased capabilities to pursue policies unpalatable to donor governments. Many NGOs have a patchy but better record of effectiveness than governments in dispensing aid. So we find that today donor governments are increasingly enlisting the active cooperation of non-state actors, especially global and transnational businesses, and development agencies.

Public funding for development NGOs now amounts to 30 per cent—including, notably, financing by the World Bank. Even human rights organizations get some state funding, especially in Europe. Thus there are not just pressures and counter-pressures. In some areas there is a degree of partnership, though funds are often given to appease public pressure. And this wary but growing cooperation between governments and many non-governmental interest groups leads both sides to modify their behaviour.

Inevitably the increasing influence of non-state actors changes the ways the actors themselves behave. In addition to the modification of NGO behaviour to accommodate both donor and recipient governments and international institutions, we can see the increasing bureaucratization of pressure groups, especially in their operations in underdeveloped states.

Sum up

Now let me try to sum up this complicated pattern of international relations—or transnational relations—in its present phase of hegemony.

By hegemony I mean the material condition of technological, economic and strategic superiority which enables a single great power or group of powers, or the great powers acting collectively, to bring such great inducements and pressures to bear that most other states lose some of their external and internal independence.

Hegemony lies in the spectrum between multiple independences and world government. I want to emphasize the continuities along the spectrum; the gradual nature of changes in transnational relations; and the mutations of the same pattern. We need to avoid sharp distinctions of either/or.

The rich developed Western democracies now enjoy a great and growing hegemonic superiority in the international system. In these countries a wide variety of transnational NGOs ranges from economic enterprises like banks and oil companies through philanthropic development agencies to vocal champions of moral causes. All three groups want to change the internal affairs of weaker and less democratic states. Transnational NGOs use what direct influence they can on the peripheral states. They also try to get their own elected governments to bring more effective state inducements and pressures to bear including, ultimately armed force. While non-governmental organizations urge governments to act in Westphalian times of non-intervention, and in times of direct administration of dependencies, they are most vociferous and most successful in times of hegemony. For hegemony combines a high capacity to subsidize and intervene with a high willingness to do so.

The governments of hegemonial donor states respond to their NGOs, and usually share their cultural assumptions about standards of civilization—what is desirable and right. But in times of hegemony, hegemonial governments want to act as far as possible by *proxy* rather than directly. So they bring inducements and pressures to bear mainly on the governments of recipient states. In extreme cases—Bosnia, Afghanistan—they *create* local governments as proxies through which to deal. And they develop wary partnerships with the more moderate NGOs, using them as proxies too.

Recipient governments want the inducements offered by donor governments and NGOs. Many find that they cannot manage without regular and continuous aid. But weak states are threatened by chaos. And the strings attached by Western donors to their aid are apt to weaken weak states still further. So most recipient governments comply with the moral demands of the developed states—standards of civilization, treatment of foreign enterprises and so on—only to the extent necessary to ensure the aid. Some see the merits of Western demands and practices more clearly than others.

And finally may I remind you that the pendulum is swinging, and that we do not know how long the present phase of Western hegemony will last.

11 The changing international system

Unpublished lecture at the University of Copenhagen, May 2001

The purpose of this paper is to examine recent developments in the long process of working out a comprehensive theory of international relations. Why do we need such a theory? I think there are two reasons:

First, it is impossible to understand any set of connected events without some general idea, a working theory, about how those events relate to one another. And as new facts are established, they either fit the theory or you must modify the theory to accommodate them.

Second, in real life, governments and ministries of foreign affairs have assumptions about how international affairs work. If they are wrong, the consequences may be serious.

When the British Committee began its work some forty years ago, there wasn't much international theory. We thought in terms of about seventy sovereign and independent states, operating in a states system, rather like the solar system. Theorists came to call this the Westphalian system. Hedley Bull led us to understand it as an anarchical society.

Some of us treated our anarchical society as unique, the only one worth studying. Other systems were interesting only when they were semi-Westphalian, like the Greek city states. But Martin Wight and I felt that a search for a general theory needed also to study systems where some or most of the political entities were not independent but in varying degrees dependent. He and I wanted especially to discuss hegemonies and suzerain systems, where some states were partially dependent but retained nominal independence and a high degree of autonomy in practice. It seemed to me that once you compared the practice of our international society with past hegemonial and imperial systems, it ceased to seem so unique and so anarchical, but appeared like those of many other historical systems. Indeed it had pronounced hegemonial characteristics, quite a way along the spectrum of possible patterns. These ideas and hunches led me to compile my *Evolution of International Society*, a comparative study of the historical evidence.

In contrast to this line of thought, the popular Zeitgeist of the decolonization age (1960–1990) relegated hegemonies and empires to "the dustbin of history", and asserted that Westphalian independent statehood was the only politically acceptable formula. The international system became less

The changing international system 93

integrated and more anarchical, and the assumptions of politicians more restricted.

So it is good to find that nevertheless a number of younger scholars in Britain, Denmark and elsewhere are producing serious comparative studies of past hegemonial and imperial systems. Michael Doyle's book *Empires* is an outstanding example. Above all there is the work of Barry Buzan and Richard Little. They effectively developed the wider perspective that Wight and I considered essential. Now we have their book *International Systems in World History*. This work seems to me a big step towards what Wight and I hoped for. It widens the study of international relations back to its beginnings in the contacts that hunter-gatherer bands found indispensable, and spells out a provisional but coherent theory for the whole set of known relations between distinct political entities.

So where are we now? The battle against anti-historical limitations on international theory has largely been won. In Buzan and Little's vivid phrase, international relations studies are out of the Westphalian straitjacket. And now that we have taken off the blinkers and look back over the historical record, what do we see? The nominal constitution of the system, as expressed in the United Nations Charter and international law, is still some two hundred separate sovereign and equal states. And most governments of these states continue to claim that it is the only acceptable system. But the practice of the system—the way it actually operates—is moving far from these Westphalian assumptions. The practice continues to outrun the conventionally accepted theory.

Now my generation must hand the torch over to younger scholars and practitioners, to ask new questions about the present system and where it stands in the context of history. Among the general questions which younger scholars should address, may I suggest the following?

1) A good first question is: What is the nature of the present system? How does it now operate in practice? There is no doubt that it is to some degree hegemonial, and increasingly integrated. Where does that put it along the theoretical spectrum between multiple independences and overarching authority?

    How much Westphalian practice still exists in the system? Not only in flags and embassies and seats at the United Nations, but also in the minds of those who conduct international relations, and in the media? In addition to Westphalian legitimacy, the current international society is sometimes described as the replacement of colonial unilateralism by a collective hegemony of the most developed Western states. Or is it rather like a series of concentric circles, with the United States wearing the imperial mantle at the centre, dealing with a periphery of failed and incompetent states and quasi-states as well as other more independent ones? All three formulas describe some aspects of the complex reality, but each is inadequate by itself.

2) A second question concerns the role of states in international relations. The three formulas in the previous paragraph—Westphalian, collective hegemony, concentric circles—assume that the principal actors in the system are still the individual member states. But perhaps something more radical is happening. The interaction of societies in an international system covers a much wider range than the interaction of states, or perhaps we should say governments. Are states losing the dominant role that we took for granted, even though they remain important?

Strategic authority and intervention—the radiation of military technology—is a job for states. The use of hegemonial force is very newsworthy. But it is occasional and localized. It is mainly used to stop warfare within peripheral states, or combat terrorism. But in the economic and cultural fields there is some erosion of the dominant role of states in the system. Economic globalization—the radial effects of economic technology—is very largely a field for private enterprise, outside governmental control. Cultural values, especially the hegemonial spread of standards of civilization, are also substantially non-governmental, concerned with the welfare of individual human beings, though states play a large role.

* * *

Let us look at these aspects of international involvement in more detail. There appear to be two main ways that the centrality of independent nation states may be weakening.

One question is how much legislative and executive power is being transferred from individual states to international institutions like the United Nations and its subsidiaries. Some people see the United Nations as a super-state entity, whose mission is to control aggression and internal chaos, and reform backward states, as well as dispense medicine, technology, financing and other benefits world-wide.

The power—the capacity to act—of the UN executive does seem to be growing. But it meets great resistance, both constitutional and practical. The founders of the United Nations were Westphalians. They constituted it as machinery which responsible states could use to act collectively. How far do the key UN organs—the Security Council, the World Bank and International Monetary Fund, even the Secretary-General—now act, not as agents of a nebulous "world community", nor to protect the independence of a majority of the two-hundred members, but as agents of those great powers willing to act? Is the shadowy authority of the United Nations essentially a figleaf of respectability for hegemonial action: through the Security Council for the use of force, and through the World Bank and International Monetary Fund for the use of money?

The other erosion of state dominance is more significant. It is due to two world-wide, continous and growing fields of interaction mentioned above:

economic integration or globalization; and linked to it cultural rules, including standards of civilization. Both operate radially, and their motive forces are largely non-governmental. In these two areas governments play an indispensable role. But not the only one; and not, I think, the most important one. How far are globalization and ethical standards eroding, and might continue to erode, not only this or that aspect of sovereignty but the basic premise of Westphalian theory, the state itself?

We in the technically and politically more developed core societies want a healthy global economy, both to sustain our own economies and from a sense of responsibility. We provide continuous world-wide coordinated help of various kinds to countries that cannot manage adequately for themselves, which make up more than half the members of our international society. The developed world operates a huge but in my opinion still inadequate and still somewhat experimental centrifuge to the periphery.

There are three main categories of aid. We provide material goods, including medical, or money to buy them. We provide technology, education, training and know-how, including expert personnel. And equally important, we provide markets in our economies for the goods that the periphery can then produce.

Donor governments play a part here. They foster globalization both directly and through international agencies like the World Bank and the International Monetary Fund which they control. But more than half the transfer of resources is purveyed or mediated by private enterprise, which expects a profit in return. Therefore so long as the peripheral states retain enough effective autonomy to bargain about the terms, the transfer of resources and skills needs to offer benefits to both parties.

The mainly Western donors also demand in return the observance of their standards of civilization. Human rights, democracy, social justice and the environment, the campaign against poverty, focus on individuals across state lines. These standards are too difficult for many peripheral states where the practical alternatives are firm government or chaos. Also governments in the periphery want more real independence than they now have. Even so, peripheral governments increasingly observe Western standards as the price of aid.

You will notice that both economic globalization and standards of civilization have distributive overtones. They are at least partially intended to operate outward to poor societies, and downward to the poor inside those societies. The trend and the distributive effects are likely to continue. So long as the economic aid continues, so will hegemonial pressures for the donors' standards of civilization. In any case the collective aid and intervention is controversial. I believe it entangles both the interveners and the intervened. It limits independence. It erodes the freedom of action, or the aloofness, of all states, even the largest, the United States. It needs further objective study.

Of course the donor societies and capitalist enterprises do not have it all their own way. There is a lot of opposition to hegemonial radiation. Some critics maintain that aid and intervention are not positive or generous enough to satisfy even Western public opinion, let alone that in recipient countries; and are not always carried out wisely or well. Sometimes they seem to be hardly done at all—look at Africa. Some of the opposition comes from leftward public opinion in the developed societies and elsewhere. Some comes from trade unions and businesses threatened by globalization and imports from the periphery. Some is resistance to hegemonial attempts to impose Western standards: this comes especially from the Islamic world, but also from China and Cuba and other dictatorships. All this opposition wants to preserve a greater role for nation states, and for the governments of states. The nature and effectiveness of anti-hegemonial resistence needs further study also.

And in a changing world may not the standards of civilization, now so Western, also change? The great Asian powers—China, Japan, India—are becoming richer and more developed. How far is their influence in the hegemonial concert likely to grow? Will they make standards of civilization, and especially concepts of justice, less exclusively Western? May the global international system become more integrated but less Euro-American? Here the historical perspective is useful. Until the nineteenth century Europeans regarded the major civilizations of Asia as in many ways more advanced than their own, and their demand for Asian goods was greater than the Asian demand for what the Europeans had to offer in return.

* * *

We live in a period of constant and profound change. International theory, and even awareness of how the practice is changing, have lagged behind the changes. There is a lot of work to do.

We need more research into hegemonial authority, globalization and aid. How do they function in practice? I believe that they are increasing.

Advanced technology has a radial effect throughout the system: strategic, economic and cultural. Strategic authority and intervention are a job for states. Economic globalization is largely implemented by private enterprise, outside governmental control, though increasingly regulated by governments. Government aid, directly and through institutions like the World Bank, remains significant. Cultural values and standards of civilization, are substantially non-governmental, and focused on individuals; but states play a large role in imposing and implementing them.

Developed Western societies now dominate the patterns of aid and intervention. They have both ethical and profitable motives. The hunger of the periphery for more equably distributed prosperity provides a lever for the West to promote both its advanced economic techniques and its cultural values. But the great powers of Asia, like China, India and Japan, are developing rapidly. How may they, and their values, influence the hegemonic structure of the system?

Note two consequences of increasing hegemony and globalization: it entangles societies, and governments, ever more with one another. And it erodes the dominance of states in the international system—makes it less of a states system.

To understand the structure of the present system requires detailed and objective research, then adjustment of the theory.

12 1878: A case study in collective hegemony

Ninteenth-century Concert of European Great Powers

The governments and policy makers of major powers locked in an international system are usually aware that the wide range of their national interests requires collaboration with various other powers on different issues at different times, and that in addition they all have other interests in common, especially the shared advantages of making the system work. Where the large powers constitute a club or class of Great Powers, with recognized special rights and responsibilities, the awareness of common advantage extends the areas in which Great Powers are willing to reach compromises on issues where their state interest in the narrow sense conflicts with that of another great power. The sense of a shared interest in the functioning of the system is not an alternative to the pursuit of a specific national interest; rather it sets limits beyond which it would not pay to push a specific disagreement. The compromises on issues affecting the Ottoman Empire reached by the Concert of Europe in 1878 provide a useful example of the process.

The European Concert developed out of, and was legitimized by, the Vienna settlement after the defeat of Napoleon, and functioned until its collapse at the beginning of the twentieth century. It inherited many of its assumptions and practices from earlier arrangements. The Concert Great Powers consisted of: Russia, Britain (then usually called England), Austria (which became Austria-Hungary), France, Prussia (which expanded into Germany) and Italy after its formation. The Concert powers made up much the greater part of the population, wealth and military capacity of Europe; and they refused to grant much say to the smaller states, or to saddle them with much responsibility outside their borders. The nineteenth-century Concert was a *collective hegemony*.

Most of the time there was more cooperation, and less confrontation and conflict, between the powers of the nineteenth-century Concert than popular assumptions and even academic histories today suggest. The operation of the Concert was a continuous process, which was able to function even during the period of limited wars in the middle of the century. The Concert was held in place to a large extent by the two "bookend powers" England on Europe's western flank and Russia on its eastern, pressing in opposite directions. For a whole century neither England nor Russia went to war on any European issue.

George Kennan described the nature and atmosphere of the Concert of Great Powers around 1878 in a draft essay that he sent to me in 1994 entitled *The Structure of the International Community*:

> "In the final years of the Victorian era, world society was marked by what could be called the semblance of an international order. It was little more than a semblance because, as we know today, it was already extensively undermined by forces seldom visible to people of that time; and it was, as the initial years of the ensuing 20th century were about to reveal, dangerously vulnerable to abuse by incompetent and frivolous statesmen. But it was not all unreal. It had certain elements of strength. And first among these was the fact that there were in those days relatively few centers of power, for the most part the great imperial and royal chanceries. This meant that the ability to affect the unfolding of world events rested in very few hands, and most of those hands were ones that derived steadiness from such sources as superior education, tradition, and, not least, a sense of personal security based, for better or for worse, on relative affluence and firm social position. This, such as it was, was the order destroyed by the two great European wars of this century and their immediate consequences."[1]

The Ottoman Empire, though partly in geographical Europe, was considered to be outside the European *grande république*, and regarded as the western theatre of the Anglo-Russian "great game" that stretched across Asia to the Pacific: a struggle where, with the one exception of the Crimean War, both powers recognized the advantage of stopping short of direct force against each other.

Unrest in European Ottoman provinces

In the 1870s the European provinces of the Ottoman Empire were in a state of ferment, especially the Greek Orthodox majority. There were riots in Bulgaria and Bosnia, and severe repression. Public opinion in Europe became concerned about Ottoman "atrocities." Particularly vociferous were those strange bedfellows, right-wing Russians in the Orthodox church and the military, and the British Liberal Party. Both wanted to drive the Ottoman Empire out of Christian Europe: Gladstone "one and all, bag and baggage" in favour of independent states, the Russians in favour of Russian protectorates. The Great Powers of the Concert saw the threat to European order posed by the unrest in the Ottoman European provinces. The six Concert governments recognized their responsibility to work out and impose a joint solution which would alleviate the suffering in Ottoman Europe and also adequately protect their own special interests.

The Ottoman authorities administered their Christian subjects through the churches. The Russian Government, which claimed that the Tsar was the protector of all Orthodox Christians, put pressure on the Ottoman Government to set up an autonomous *Exarchate of Bulgaria* independent of the Patriarch at Constantinople and covering all Ottoman territory in Europe where Orthodox Christians were in a majority and opted for it. To balance this extension of Russian influence, in 1877 Russia agreed with Austria on Austrian control of Bosnia to stop atrocities there. Then in 1878 Russia invaded Bulgaria, and at the bilateral treaty of San Stefano forced the Ottomans to agree to full Bulgarian independence, including an outlet on the Mediteranean. The other Concert powers agreed that Ottoman repression must be stopped, but declared that the Russian formula was unacceptably unilateral. Especially England, led by Prime Minister Disraeli, wanted to keep Russia out of the Mediterranean.

Congress of Berlin

After some preliminary negotiation, the German Chancellor Bismarck invited the Concert powers and the Ottomans to what we would call a summit conference in Berlin. There he undertook a detailed exploration of what responsibilities the Concert should collectively assume for ensuring standards of civilization in the Ottoman domains, and what strategic compromises both Russia and England could be brought to accept. The real negotiations were highly personal: Bismarck would dine one night "en famille" with the Russian minister Gorchakov, with the conversation in Russian; and a following night with Disraeli, with the conversation in English. Bismarck did not want anything specific for Germany in the Ottoman provinces; he wanted to remain on good terms with both England and Russia, and therefore to prevent a quarrel between them which could oblige him to take sides and so disrupt the European order.

The result of the negotiations was the Treaty of Berlin, hailed as an international "charter for the Balkans."

The principal decision of the Congress on standards of civilization in Ottoman Europe was that the territorial integrity of the empire should be preserved, but that the administration of certain disturbed areas should be taken out of Ottoman hands and entrusted to one or more Concert powers. Specific arrangements were as follows: Bulgaria was reduced in size, cut off from the Mediterranean and divided into two provinces. North Bulgaria was accorded wide autonomy but within the Ottoman Empire, under Prince Alexander von Battenberg a relative of both Queen Victoria and the Tsar, assisted by Russian advisers and a Russian military presence. Southern Bulgaria (called Eastern Rumelia) was accorded less autonomy, with Ottoman troops and undertakings for good governance.

England seconded the Russian agreement that Austria should administer Ottoman Bosnia Herzegovina under a European "mandate."

1878: A case study in collective hegemony 101

The Concert powers agreed to produce (and later imposed) a detailed constitution for unruly Ottoman Crete, balancing Greeks and Moslems. Later the island was divided into four zones each occupied by a Concert power (England, Russia, France, Italy) with the capital Candia divided into four quarters.

Under a separate *Cyprus Convention* the Ottomans were induced by Disraeli to invite England to use Cyprus as a base or "place d'armes" within Ottoman sovereignty, to support the empire (against Russia). England was to administer the island and pay rent in gold equivalent to some L8m a year in modern value.

The Ottomans also originally promised "necessary *reforms* elsewhere in consultation with its ally." But at Berlin the Concert relieved England of that unilateral responsibility and required the Ottomans to report on reforms in the rest of their empire to all the Concert powers, who would "supervise their implementation." This arrangement achieved only limited practical results, but was a milestone in the concept of collective responsibility.

The powers also induced the Ottomans to cede to Russia some minor disputed areas in the *Caucasus*, as the compensation for the withdrawal of Russian troops from Bulgaria.

Collective hegemonial practice

We may note in the behaviour of the European Concert in 1878 three hallmarks of collective hegemony:

1) *Prudence*. The powers put expediency above abstract principles. For instance they preserved the nominal sovereignty of the Ottoman Empire in Europe, but undertook varying forms of administrative responsibility in different provinces. The arrangements made at Berlin were in response to the pressures of the moment: they were not expected to be permanent.
2) *Moral Obligation*. The Concert powers were willing to assume collective responsibility, especially for human rights. At the Berlin Congress the other powers regarded both Russia and England as too unilateral.
3) The powers aimed to impose European *standards of civilization*, in which they sincerely believed, on what they regarded as a non-European state.

We may also note striking resemblances as well as differences with the present practice of the larger powers in the same areas. The Ottoman Empire of 1878 included Bosnia, Kosovo, Macedonia and Cyprus as well as Iraq, Israel, Palestine, Kuwait, and Qatar where the United States now rents a "place d'armes" or base. The four-power occupation of Crete foreshadowed the similar occupation of Germany and Austria after World War Two. The continuities illustrate the way that local problems survive in modified guises through considerable changes in the structute of the international system.

102   *1878: A case study in collective hegemony*

Even so, what matters for the study of hegemony and interstate relations is not the details of the settlement. The Concert of Europe was culturally and socially much more homogeneous than the present very diverse major powers. The events of 1878 throw an instructive light on the nature and the functioning of that remarkable institution, the European Concert, and on the wider idea of the collective responsibility of Great Powers.

13 Hegemony & History

For half a century I have been trying to think through the role of hegemony and of great powers in the structuring of international systems, and how the evidence of the past can illuminate this operation. How can both the present and the past help us towards a general theory of international politics, which was the stated objective of the British Committee?[1] There is a good deal of past evidence: particularly from European practice, but also from more distant systems. How far is it possible to assemble the past and present evidence in a way that distinguishes those features that all hegemonic systems have in common—the features that make them a set—from the characteristics limited to one or a few systems? Could such an understanding of hegemony form part of a comprehensive theory of international relations?

If the evidence is to produce valid results, it is above all necessary to look at each system, and indeed each phase of each system, on its own terms and not through the distorting lens of present assumptions. We must not project the answers into our questions. It is not easy to avoid this astigmatism, and to see how distinctive each past system was, and what the unconscious assumptions of past actors may have been. The Irish poet, Louis MacNeice, a teacher of the Greek classics, put the problem of understanding the ancient Greeks in stark language:

> "And how one can imagine oneself among them
> I do not know;
> It was all so unimaginably different
> And all so long ago."[2]

Nevertheless it is possible to distil an adequate understanding of how hegemonies work by restricting the enquiry to a limited range of specific questions about the functioning of hegemony in the relations between states that compose a system, and between the communities which the states administer and represent.

* * *

Let us look first at relations between states. States and communities vary very greatly in size and development, and therefore in influence. In systems of states towards the multiple independences end of the spectrum the influence of the strongest powers is usually called hegemonial. Theoretically a system of independent states could exist whose members all have equal size and influence; and this is a useful postulate marking the beginning or end of a series, like nought and infinity in mathematics. But every system in recorded history contains one or more large powers whose influence outweighs that of the rest. We may say therefore that in practice some degree of hegemony is always present in the multiple independences side of the spectrum. Indeed the hegemonic effect—the consequences of discrepancy in size and influence—is not an aberration but a characteristic of the area between the theoretical absolute of multiple independences on the one hand and the area where the system becomes so tight, and hegemonic influence so strong, that it merges into suzerainty. In the transitional area there are tacit suzerainties which retain some features of hegemony.

Hegemonic influence can modify the behaviour of other states, and the system itself, in a wide range of ways. The use of force, and by extension the ability to coerce, has been traditionally associated with hegemony, and is one conspicuous way to exercise hegemonic influence. But it is not the only one. Economic strength, exemplified in many systems by the power and influence of mercantile cities and states, is perhaps equally important. When for instance Sforza, the ruler of Milan, expressed to the Medici in Florence his fear that the Venetian merchant oligarchy might become the "signori di tutta Italia", he was thinking of Venice's economic strength (which enabled them to buy military power) and the appeal of the Venetian rule of law.[3]

The principal effect of hegemonic influence is to induce other states and communities in the system to conform more closely to the purposes and practices of the hegemonic power, or in certain cases (for instance that discussed in the preceding chapter) to accept the compromises worked out by a joint hegemony.

Some mild forms of hegemony may be little more than attempts to control the functioning of the system itself: that is, the external policies of other states in the system. But in practice hegemonic pressures quickly extend to the internal affairs of other communities, such as religion and social structure.

The converse is also true. Hegemonic influence is constrained and limited by the rules and institutions of any organized system, and more strongly by an international society whose rules are reinforced by shared codes of conduct and beliefs. Hegemonic pressures inside a system inevitably provoke some degree of anti-hegemonial resistance. The usual response to the hegemonic challenge (as Toynbee would say) is the formation of an anti-hegemonial alliance or coalition, which marshals the opposition and so makes resistance more effective than if its members act alone. I know of no single hegemonic power (as opposed to collective hegemonies) that has not provoked a significant degree of anti-hegemonial resistance or coordinated opposition, though this may fall well short of a military alliance, let alone war. Both the pressures and the counter-pressures must be reckoned as effects of hegemony on a states system.

One theory of the balance of power suggests that a hegemony will generate enough anti-hegemonial resistance to counterbalance it. That was the case in Europe since the Thirty Years War: the settlements of Westphalia, Utrecht, Vienna and Versailles marked anti-hegemonial victories. But in other systems a hegemonic power has frequently been able to establish a dominion or even empire over the whole system. The standard example is the Roman Republic's steady enforcement of control over the Macedonian/ Hellenistic world.

At present there is a debate about how effective the US hegemony really is, despite its greatly superior capacity to use force. Force, even as a last resort, is apt to have unpredictable consequences. The United States seems to be learning, from recent experience and from the pressures of economics and what has been called "soft balancing",[4] that it can reach its overall objectives more effectively by diplomacy, expediency and prudence. Indeed in some major areas such as East Asia and the Western Pacific the United States contributes to regional balance rather than threatens it; and the other major powers of the area, China, Japan and Russia, all apparently want the US presence there to continue.

Since the animators of an anti-hegemonial coalition need to solicit rather than constrain support from other members of the system, their alliance will be more egalitarian than that of a hegemonic power and its client allies. If they succeed in pulling down the hegemonic power, as they often do, the new rules, institutions and practices that they then put in place will reflect the egalitarian and anti-hegemonic practices of their alliance. The Westphalian settlement of 1648[5] is the classic example of this tendency.

Anti-hegemonial resistance is an integral feature of a mono-hegemonic system because pressure generates counter-pressure, rather than because a system based on multiple independences for sovereigns is more natural or more morally desirable than a more integrated or centralized system. The ostensible purpose of anti-hegemonial coalitions is to protect weak states against strong ones. But the animators of anti-hegemonial coalitions are states or rulers that are themselves unable to dominate their system and are willing to take risks to prevent another power from doing so. Conspicuous historical examples are: the Corinthians and their daughter polis the Syracusans, who consistently supported the weaker side in the see-saw of conflicts between Greek states or in the case of Syracuse the fluctuating struggle of Rome and Carthage;[6] and the Netherlands which pursued the same elastic and dangerous policy between the Habsburgs and France.[7]

The most sophisticated form of anti-hegemonialism, which evolved to its full extent apparently only in Westphalian Europe, is the balance of power. This much discussed concept was developed by the rulers of Europe and their advisers, designed to prevent one hegemony from succeeding another and to anchor their society of sovereigns permanently as near the anarchical end of the spectrum as possible (though they did not use this terminology). Not only the Westphalian but also the Utrecht settlement with its insistence on a "just balance", and that of Vienna were explicitly anti-hegemonial; and the same tone pervades the Covenant of the League of Nations and to a lesser extent the United Nations Charter. The balance seems originally to have been a banker's concept. It was used by the Medici in Florence in answer to Sforza's initiative mentioned above to destroy the hegemonial power of Venice. The Medici understood that when one hegemonial threat was destroyed, another was all too quick to replace the vacuum. If the affairs of Italy, and indeed all Europe, could be "in some way balanced", weakening Venice only just enough to ensure that its hegemony was not replaced by another, then every ruler could be independent.[8] During the eighteenth century the "just balance" stipulated by the Utrecht settlement was in fact achieved and maintained by a series of shifting alliances and minor wars of adjustment.[9]

A single hegemon or a diarchy does not normally find all smaller states ranged against it. It can count on some client allies or coalitions of the willing. The policy of these client allies is not normally determined by preference for a tighter, more hegemonial structure of their states system. It is rather conditioned by traditions of mutual support, local issues and enemies, and a desire for aid and subsidies. Earlier hegemonies, as well as the present US one, have conformed to this pattern. Examples from classical Greece are Plataea, animated by opposition to the Thebans, and Argos by opposition to the Spartans;[10] and from the European system the support of the rulers of Bavaria and Cologne for the hegemonial policies of France.[11] In ancient China the pro-hegemonial policy of the state of Zheng[12] seems to have been systematic, the opposite of Corinthian and Dutch policy.

The role of hegemony in the working of international systems comprises not only the fairly straightforward effect of the individual hegemony of a single state, or concentration of power such as the Habsburg family's collection of states. There is also the collective hegemony of a small number of great powers.[13] This more subtle form of hegemony usually involves all the stronger states in the system. Collective hegemony is perhaps principally a hegemonial reaction against the anarchic anti-hegemonial demand for independent sovereignties which the balance of power is intended to perpetuate. It certainly has in it a sense of balance, born perhaps of the fact that collective hegemonies tend to form after successful opposition to mono-hegemonies. But while collective hegemons check and balance one another to maintain a certain equilibrium in the system, they also and more importantly collaborate to establish arrangements and policies which they agree are desirable or are willing to accept. In these circumstances they often deliberate and act without much regard for the views of other states. Little describes the expedient side of it well as "the great powers bargaining to reach a consensual outcome that optimizes their various interests."[14] The alternative term for a collective hegemony, "associative balance of power", seems to me to lay too much stress on the element of competition and balance. The statesmen who have operated joint hegemonies have usually been animated less by a wary suspicion of each other than by awareness of the expediency of *raison de système*, and also, significantly, a shared belief in certain moral obligations.

The nineteenth-century European states, ostensibly a Westphalian anarchical society, in fact functioned as a collective hegemony. After the fall of Napoleon, Tsar Alexander proposed an extreme form of collective hegemony, which he called a Holy Alliance of rulers committed to manage the European society of states in accordance with certain moral principles. The powers later settled for the much looser Concert of Europe favoured especially by England. The functioning of the Concert in its later stages is illustrated by the example in Chapter 9. The incorporation of Asia and Africa into the European system, described in *The Expansion of International Society* edited by Bull and myself, provides a broader example of collective hegemony. The European powers concerned expanded into the two continents in competition with one another, as they had in the previous century. But they no longer resorted to almost continuous force, state and private, against each other: they operated within a framework of agreements and bargains, and began the joint hegemonic imposition of their rules, institutions and values on the Asians and Africans. Two striking examples of the collective European hegemony operating beyond its borders are the conference in Berlin in 1884 which partitioned sub-Saharan Africa, and the joint use of force in China in 1900.

I first grasped the idea of a collective hegemony operating behind a facade of multiple independences when serving as a junior member of the British team in the long US/UK/Soviet negotiations in the Kremlin in 1945 on, among other things, a new international order—or as Bull would put it, reshaping the rules and institutions of international society. Molotov proposed that the new United Nations should be a hegemonial organization of the three great powers. When they agreed they would act together to keep other states in order; but the United Nations would not be able to deal with disagreements between the three. One could hear echoes of Tsar Alexander's holy alliance. However Molotov also proposed an international order which was in many other respects one of nominally independent states. Did the legitimacy of his proposed international order match his proposed hegemonial practice? The clear answer was No. It seemed to me little more than a figleaf of respectability over naked three power rule. Whether Molotov believed that the tripartite hegemony he outlined would actually operate I do not know; I suspect not. In any case with the onset of the Cold War the new order quickly resolved itself into two opposed hegemonic systems, just as the end of that struggle led to the current order of US hegemonial power and its corresponding discontents.

* * *

When we turn to non-state actors, and the individual human beings whose welfare is increasingly a focus of international concern, we find their roles in hegemonial systems less clear cut, and less understood, than that of governments. Until recently the conventional view of international relations was of dealings between sovereign and substantially independent states: little more than diplomatic history. But students of the subject have become increasingly aware that relations between governments are only part of the picture, and in the present phase a shrinking part. They pay more attention to the role of all transnational actors. The powerful economic links of trade; the pressures of religious bodies, especially the extreme and fanatical ones; charitable non-governmental organizations that support world obedience to their moral standards; private medical and educational enterprises; the internet; and other individual activities all play their parts in knitting the international system together. The fitful but continuing globalization of the world jumps over state boundaries and interweaves what were previously more separate communities.

The macrohistorian William McNeill[15] and others have suggested that the determining feature of the development of the human race is the spread of technology. Technological success induces neighbours to accept or borrow other features, too, from the more developed community, ranging from manufacturing techniques and political organization to religion, culture and the arts. Values ride on the back of techniques that are copied by non-state actors. Such radial influence can either be exercised by conquest, or it can respect the nominal independence and a very considerable degree of autonomy of recipient communities.

As early as January 1965 Desmond Williams brought the hegemonic consequences of uneven technological development to the attention of the British Committee.

> A crucial consideration, which has special reference to the present day, is that technological and economic advance are calculated perhaps to divide rather than unite. They do not in themselves provide a secure basis for world co-operation, and sooner or later become more effective in the generation of rivalry. It is arguable that they set forces in operation which tend to produce rather a World-Empire.[16]

New standards of civilization, like advances in technology, have for more than a century been, and are still, largely generated in the developed West. In sub-Saharan Africa for instance, during the first half of the twentieth century, parallel unilateral colonizers imposed dependent states on the European model. Unilateral colonization was on balance an unsatisfactory result of hegemonial predominance; but in retrospect it seems overdenigrated. Most of the difficulties occurred in areas of European settlement.

Hegemony & History 109

Colonial administrators in non-settler colonies usually showed a considerable sense of moral concern for the welfare and development of their "charges." This sense of responsibility was often, though alas certainly not always, reflected in the policies and priorities of the imperial governments. Commercial developoment and exploitation, which had been the primary motive for non-settler expansion in the first place, continued to be largely left to the private sector.

Decolonization[17] brought questions of the moral obligations of all developed communities to the fore. Development according to Western criteria is now a collective responsibility, spread hegemonially and partly paid for by governmental and private agencies in the developed world.[18] Semi-autonomous instruments of collective hegemony funded by donor states, like the World Bank and the International Monetary Fund, require recipient governments to conform to certain standards as the price of aid. So we have the concept of international civil servants exercising a collective hegemonial influence on weak states that turn to them for help.

These long term tendencies, along with the increasing focus on individuals, all add up to the erosion of the centrality of the independent state; both in practice as the pivotal operator of the world system, and in the minds of those searching for a comprehensive international theory. What once were systems of separate and independent states that could be plausibly compared to the solar system, now seem increasingly to be changing into interdependent communities of individuals locked together in "Spaceship Earth."

Nevertheless we must not underestimate the role of states in a more hegemonic and integrated world, if the pendulum continues to swing that way. The caveat is especially necessary in the nebulous area of the reponsibility of the governments of developed countries for the material wellbeing and human rights of individuals in states whose governments are unable or unwilling to ensure acceptable standards. Recipient governments will become increasingly agents of policies devised and paid for outside their area of administration. In the present range along the spectrum, the government of even a very weak state can refuse to accept or to implement the terms of aid offered by the hegemonial authorities. But insofar as recipient states accept the packages offered to them, both the governmental and private sectors of such states will act as conveyor belts for the hegemonic shaping of the system, as well as, often enough, contributing to anti-hegemonic resistance. At the other end of the scale, great powers like Russia, China and the United States still see themselves as independent states pursuing their national interests rather than as members of a collective hegemony, though their statesmen often act more collectively and hegemonially than they talk and perhaps think.

Many policy makers and observers consider that the centrality of independent nation states is eroding differently in Europe. Erosion there has certainly been faster than anywhere else. As Vaclav Klaus, President of the Czech Republic, put it: "The acceleration of integration during the past twenty years has been realised by a gradual but systematic undermining of the former inter-governmental nature of relations between countries."[19] European integrationists fear the anarchy and nationalist passions that led to two catastrophic wars in the first half of the twentieth century; and they are conscious that their *grande république* is a cultural as well as geographic unity, with shared beliefs and attitudes. They welcome their Union coming together. However they want to achieve union, not by hegemonic pressure that might develop into a Napoleonic dominion, but by negotiation between equals, developing common institutions in which each member is proportionally represented, and to which various elements of sovereignty are transferred in stages from the member states. They hope integration will continue until perhaps some new form of confederacy of the willing is reached, endowed with a common foreign and defence policy and able to act internationally for practical purposes as a single federation. Nations like France or Lithuania will of course continue to exist, but the "Europeanists" hope that national governments will be progressively limited to provincial autonomy and to implementing decisions taken at the centre.

In this process, and the resulting Union, hegemonic and anti-hegemonic influences would take different forms from those in nominally independent states. But the evidence is that they will still operate. One much-discussed form is a dyarchy of the two most powerful nations, France and Germany; and other patterns of pressure will also be present, including the influence of non-state actors and of public opinion. There is an instructive resemblance between national governments implementing decisions of the central institutions of the European Union and the relation of recipient governments to donor states and institutions on the wider world stage. We should also note the radial hegemonial influence exerted by the European Union on states that want to join it: what Ole Wæver aptly calls silent disciplining. A comprehensive theory must allow for developments of this kind.

Europe is a special case, held together by both the beliefs and preferences of a substantially common culture. But what held in some sort of order the very diverse and nominally independent member states of Bull's anarchical world-wide society, as the British Committee started to look at it in the 1960s? What seemed to us the equivalent of gravity in the solar system? Butterfield and Wight suggested prudence and moral obligation: the equivalents of Wendt's calculation and belief. These restraints worked adequately most of the time; but they were not enough to prevent the destructive chaos of the previous half century in Europe and East Asia. What held previous anarchical systems together? Our understanding of this area is still very incomplete. We need more research into what—or lack of what—leads to chaos.

* * *

This, then, is how I see the nature of hegemony. It is an integral and characteristic feature of systems near the anarchic end of the spectrum. The influence of the hegemonic power or powers provides some coherence and structure to what would otherwise be an amorphous conglomerate. Hegemonic powers and their client allies exert their influence by pressures and inducements, broadly in support of order and to induce other states to conform more closely to their principles and practices. In this they are backed by those non-state actors whose interests lie in the same direction. Hegemonic pressure generates opposition; and the opponents tend to form anti-hegemonial coalitions, which coordinate and harmonize a corresponding structure of counter inducements and pressures. The anti-hegemonial counterstructure is likely to be strengthened by the rules and practices put in place by the members of an inter-state system, which usually have an anti-hegemonial purpose. The coalition will also receive the support of those non-state actors that favour freedom of action.

The pattern is somewhat more complex in the case of collective hegemonies. Some of the influence and inducements of the hegemonic partners are used laterally, so to speak, to achieve compromises and agreed purposes among themselves, rather than directed exclusively towards third parties; and the lines of anti-hegemonial resistance are also weaker and less coordinated. Within this general hegemonic structure there is usually plenty of room for states or communities that stand outside entangling alliances and the donor–recipient framework, states that neither give nor receive.

Together these pressures produce a dynamic equilibrium of structure that is subject to continuous change. If the structure gets stronger and the lines of influence more coherent, the system becomes more integrated and moves along the spectrum towards dominion or confederacy. If the structure gets weaker and the lines of coherence become more tenuous, the system moves towards the anarchical end of the spectrum. But the evidence of history suggests that the structural lines and the general pattern of a system are likely to remain more or less the same when one state replaces another in the hegemonial position.

After half a century of looking at hegemony in the light of international systems in world history, I have concluded that the whole range of known historical systems that lies between the suzerainty of an imperial power and the theoretical absolute of real independence for all member states operates hegemonically; and this hegemonial operation has certain well-defined characteristics that appear in local guise in all the various historical systems of nominally independent states.

Notes

1 Introduction: A voyage of exploration

1. The fullest and most useful study of the work of this committee is Vigezzi (2005). Professor Vigezzi was formerly Professor of Modern and Contemporary History at the University of Milan and President of the International Commission on the History of International Relations. As an active member and sometime chairman of the British Committee on the Theory of International Politics, I can testify to the completeness and perceptiveness of this remarkable reconstruction.
2. Wight (1966: 17–24).
3. For Voltaire and Heeren on the cultural distinction between what we called a system and a society, see Watson (1992: 208–9).
4. The passages from Voltaire, de Vattel and Heeren mentioned in the previous note also reflect this contradiction.
5. Buzan (2004: 9).
6. Butterfield's views are set out in his masterly paper for the Committee (1966).
7. Bull (1977: 13).
8. Bull and Watson (1984).
9. Vigezzi, op. cit. (2005: 242).
10. Vigezzi, op. cit. (2005: 418).
11. Buzan and Little (2000).
12. Watson (1997).

2 The British Committee on the Theory of International Politics

1. Dunne (1998).
2. Watson (1992).
3. Buzan and Little (2000).
4. Higgins (1984: 42).

3 Martin Wight and the Theory of International Relations

1. Wight (1977: 21–46).
2. Butterfield and Wight (1966: 17–24). The texts of the essays written for the Committee are available in the library of the Royal Institute of International Affairs, Chatham House, St James's Square, London SW1.
3. Wight (1977: 22).
4. Butterfield (1975).
5. Wight (1977: 23–24).
6. ibid.

Notes

7. Bull (1977: 12–14).
8. Wight (1977: 42–46).
9. ibid. 44.
10. Claude (1989).
11. Higgins (1984: 42).

4 Hedley Bull, states systems and international societies

1. Bull (1977: 10).
2. ibid. 13.
3. Bull and Watson (1984).
4. Watson (1983: 95).
5. Bull (1977: 13).
6. Heeren (1834: 7, 8).
7. Bull (1977: 13).
8. Best (1985).

6 Justice between states

1. The best modern book on this subject that I know is Professor Hedley Bull's *The Anarchical Society*, 1977.
2. St Augustine (IV: 4).

8 "The Practice Outruns the Theory"

1. Butterfield and Wight (1966: 13).
2. Gong (1984).
3. Watson (1992: 316).
4. ibid. 307.

9 The future of the Westphalian anti-hegemonial international system

Many of the ideas in this paper are discussed in greater detail in Watson (1997).

12 1878: A case study in collective hegemony

1. For a discussion of this theme in the British Committee, please see my circular letter of our meeting at Bellagio in September 1974: text in Vigezzi, op.cit. (2005: 420–1).

13 Hegemony & History

1. The fullest and most useful study of the work of the committee is Vigezzi, op.cit. (2005).
2. MacNeice (1964: 60).
3. Watson, op. cit. (1992: 161).
4. Those interested in the debate about hard and soft balancing should see Paul, Wirtz and Fortman (2004).
5. Watson, op. cit. (1992: chapter 17).
6. ibid. chapter 5 and p.97.
7. ibid., chapter 17, especially p.191.
8. ibid., chapter 14.
9. ibid., chapter 18.
10. ibid., chapter 5.

11. ibid, chapters 17, 18 and 20.
12. ibid., p.88.
13. ibid., chapter 21.
14. Little (2006).
15. See for instance chapters 1 and 2 of McNeill (1974).
16. For full record of Williams' statement, see minutes of British Committee in Brunello Vigezzi, op.cit. (2005: 404–6).
17. Among the pressures that induced conservative West European statesmen like Macmillan and de Gaulle to sail with the wind of change we may note: anti-colonial public opinion in the home country and around the world; the terms of the League mandate and United Nations trustee systems, which set the goal of development to independence; and latterly in the case of France, giving colonial populations the vote for representatives in the French legislature.

    There was also the once potent argument that the maintenance of law and order, development of infrastructure, literacy in the colonizers' language and so on in order to produce wealth was not necessarily in the best interest of a colony, even where a considerable portion of that wealth was used for the benefit of the colonized. That argument has lost its edge as a result of the sharp deterioration of sub-Saharan Africa since decolonization.
18. This process is described further in chapter 7 of Watson (1997).
19. Financial Times [to follow].

Bibliography

Best, G. (1985) *The Times Literary Supplement*, February 1.
Bull, H. (1977) *The Anarchical Society: A Study of Order in World Politics*, London: Macmillan.
Bull, H. and Watson, A. (1984) *The Expansion of International Society*, Oxford: Clarendon Press.
Butterfield, H. (1966) 'The Balance of Power,' in H. Butterfield and M. Wight (eds) *Diplomatic Investigations*, London: George Allen & Unwin Ltd.
Butterfield, H. 'Raison d'Etat: The Relations between Morality and Government,' The First Martin Wight Memorial Lecture, University of Sussex, 23 April 1975.
Butterfield, H. 'The Historic States System,' unpublished paper held in the library of the Royal Institute of International Affairs, Chatham House, St. James's Square, London.
Buzan, B. (2000) 'The Theory and Practice of Power in International Relations: Past and Future,' in J.V. Ciprut (ed) *The Art of the Feud: Reconceptualizing International Relations*, Westport, CT: Praeger.
Buzan, B. (2004) *From International to World Society? English School Theory and the Social Structure of Globalization*, Cambridge: Cambridge University Press.
Buzan, B. and Little, R. (1994) 'The Idea of International System: Theory Meets History,' *International Political Science Review*, 15(3): 31–56.
Buzan, B. and Little, R. (1996) 'Reconceptualizing Anarchy: Structural Realism Meets World History,' *European Journal of International Relations*, 2(4): 403–438.
Buzan, B. and Little, R. (2000) *International Systems in World History*, Oxford: Oxford University Press.
Claude, I.L. (1962) *Power and International Relations*, New York: Random House.
Claude, I.L. (1989) Letter to Adam Watson.
Claude, I.L. (2001) Letter to Adam Watson, 29 November.
Declaration of Colonial Rights: Resolutions of the First Continental Congress, 14 October 1774.
Doyle, M.W. (1986) *Empires*, Ithaca, NY:Cornell University Press.
Dunne, T. (1998) *Inventing International Society: A History of English School*, London: Macmillan.
Gong, G.W. (1984) *The Standard of 'Civilisation' in International Society*, Oxford: Clarendon Press.
Grotius, H. (1625) *De iure belli ac pacis*, trans. A. C. Campbell, London, 1814.
Heeren, A. (1800) *Geschichte des europäischen Staatensystems*, Göttingen.

Heeren, A. (1834) *Manual of the History of the Political System of Europe & its Colonies*, vol.1, 1st edn. Oxford: DA Talboys; 2nd edn. London: Henry G. Bohn, 1846; 3rd edn. (ibid), 1873.

Higgins, R. (1984) 'Intervention and International Law' in H. Bull (ed) *Intervention in World Politics*, Oxford: Oxford University Press.

Kennan, G. (1994) 'The Structure of the International Community,' unpublished essay.

Klaus, V. (2005) 'Why Europe Must Reject Centralisation,' *Financial Times*, August 30 <http://www.hrad.cz/cms/en/prezident_cr/klaus_projevy/2573.shtml>

Little, R. (2006) 'The Balance of Power and Great Power Management' in R. Little and J. Williams (eds) *The Anarchical Society in a Globalized World*, Basingstoke, UK: Palgrave Macmillan.

MacNeice, L. (1964) *Selected Poems*, London: Faber.

McNeill, W.H. (1974) *The Shape of European History*, Oxford: Oxford University Press.

Merriam-Webster's Collegiate Dictionary (2003) 11th edn., Springfield, MA: Merriam-Webster.

The New York Times (1992) January 30.

Paul, T.V., Wirtz J.J. and Fortman, M. (eds) (2004) *Balance of Power Theory and Practice in the 21st Century*, Palo Alto, CA: Stanford University Press.

Rana, A.P. (1993) 'The New Northern Concert of Powers in a World of Multiple Interdependencies,' in K. Ajuha, H. Coppens and H. van der Wusten (eds) *Regime Transformations and Global Realignments*, London: Sage.

Rana, A.P. (1996) 'Understanding International Conflict in the Third World: A Conceptual Enquiry,' *International Studies*, 33(2): 131–154.

Rana, A.P. (2004) 'Globalisation and the Security Problematic of "Evolving" States in the Developing World,' in R. Harshe (ed.) *Interpreting Globalisation: Perspectives in International Relations*, New Delhi: Rawat Publishers.

Rosenau, J. (1990) *Turbulence in World Politics*, Princeton University Press, Princeton.

St. Augustine (1963) The City of God, vol.2, Loeb Classical Library, trans. W.M. Green, Cambridge, MA: Harvard.

St. Thomas Aquinas (1947) *Summa Theologica, Benziger Bros. edition*, Christian Classics Ethereal Library [website] (accessed 27 July 2006), http://www.ccel.org/a/aquinas/summa/SS/SS040.html#SSQ40OUTP1

Thucydides (1910) *The Peloponnesian War*, London: J. M. Dent; New York: E. P. Dutton.

de Vattel, E. (1852) *The law of nations, or, Principles of the law of nature, applied to the conduct and affairs of nations and sovereigns*, Philadelphia: T. & J.W. Johnson & Co.

Vigezzi, B. (2005) *The British Committee on the Theory of International Politics 1954–1985: The Rediscovery of History*, Milano: Edizioni Unicopli.

Voltaire, *Siècle De Louis XIV* Chapter 2

Waever, O. and Neumann, I.B. (1997) (eds) *The Future of International Relations: Masters in the Making?*, London: Routledge.

Watson, A. (1983) *Diplomacy: The Dialogue between States*, London: Eyre Methuen.

Watson, A. (1992) *The Evolution of International Society: A Comparative Historical Analysis*, London: Routledge.

Watson, A. (1997) *The Limits of Independence*, London: Routledge.
Wight, M. (1966) 'Why is there no International Theory?' in H. Butterfield and M. Wight (eds) *Diplomatic Investigations*, London: George Allen & Unwin Ltd.
Wight, M. (1977) *Systems of States*, H. Bull (ed), Leicester: Leicester University Press.

Index

absolute independence 19, 21, 111
administration 68–9, 71–2, 78, 84, 86–7, 90, 100, 103, 109
Adriatic 8
Afghanistan 90
Africa 37, 68, 70–1, 74, 96, 107–8
African Department 5
agitation 86–7
agriculture 86
ahistoricism 5
aid 6, 12–13, 44, 49, 60–2
   agencies 44
   change 95–6
   future 65, 71–3, 76
   hegemony 83–5, 88–9, 91, 106, 109
   strings 82
Aleppo 28
Alexander the Great 18, 33
Alexander, Tsar 107
alliances 20, 48–9, 55–6, 105–7, 111
Alps 8
altruism 50
Amazonia 57
ambassadors 56–7
America 8, 19, 25, 29–30, 37
   future 67
   integration 49, 51
   role 58
   standards 96
American Revolution 51
The Anarchical Society 18, 27, 29, 31, 35–7, 70, 81
anarchical society 1–3, 5–7, 9–11, 13, 26, 65, 70, 92, 106, 110
anarchophilia 5, 12, 72, 84
anarchy 67, 110
Anaximander 41
Angola 25, 59
Annan, K. 71
anti-hegemonial coalitions 4, 6

anarchical society 36
   changes 96
   future 65–79
   integration 51
   international relations 18, 23–4
   practice 54–6
   role 82, 104–6, 109, 111
   states systems 28
Aramaic 16
arbitrators 40
Argos 106
Aristotle 41
armed conflict 76, 79
armed forces 12, 90
arms control 78
Armstrong, W. 7
Arthashastra 18
Asia 13, 28, 37, 48–9, 58
   hegemony 96, 99, 107
   resurgence 64, 67–70, 72, 74
Athenians 20, 25, 55–7
Atlantic 67
Augustus, Emperor 20, 55–6
Australians 35
Austria 98, 100–1
Austria-Hungary 98
autarchy 60

balance of power 4, 17–19, 23–4, 43, 61, 82, 105–7
Balkans 8
banks 7, 76, 83, 85, 90, 106
Battenberg, A. von 100
Bavaria 106
Berlin, Congress of 100–1, 107
Berlin, Treaty of 100
Best, G. 34
Bismarck, O. von 100
bookend powers 98
Bosnia 78, 85, 90, 99–101

Brazil 29
Britain 28, 37, 44, 72, 93, 98–9, 107
British Committee on the Theory of International Politics 1–5, 7
　anarchical society 35, 37
　changes 92
　hegemony 103, 108, 110
　practice 81
　role 10–14
　states systems 27
British Foreign Office 1, 4–5, 61
British Raj 15, 21
Bulgaria 99–101
Bull, H. 3–4, 11, 14, 16–17, 26–37, 46, 54, 70, 81, 85, 92, 107, 110
bureaucracy 75, 90
Burke, E. 28, 32, 41
Bush, G. 58
Butterfield, H. 1–4, 6, 11, 14, 18, 20, 23, 36, 50, 58, 76, 110
Buzan, B. 1, 3, 5, 8, 10–12, 66, 81, 93

Cameroon 77
Canada 72
capital 75
capitalism 89, 95
capitulations 16–17, 28, 32
Caribbean 61, 70
Carthage 105
Castro, F. 48
Catholics 6, 42
Caucasus 101
Central Asia 57
Chatham House 18
China 12–13, 15, 17, 25, 30, 32
　change 96
　future 66–9, 72–4, 77
　hegemony 105–7, 109
　integration 46–7
　justice 40
　practice 56, 60
Chinese 44
Chou En-Lai 37, 48
Christendom 41
Christians 16, 28, 41, 99–100
churches 38, 40, 99–100
city states 58, 67, 92
civil society 85
Claude, I. 19, 65, 83–5
coalitions of the willing 106
codes of conduct 2–3, 15–16, 29
　future 71
　hegemony 104
　integration 46, 50

justice 39
　practice 54, 62
　states systems 31
coercion 2, 21–2, 56, 104
Cold War 13, 42, 48–9, 52, 59, 67, 70, 107
collective economic security 61–3, 71
Cologne 106
colonization 12, 36, 42–4, 47
　change 93
　future 67, 69–71
　hegemony 108–9
　practice 57, 84–7
Commanders of the Faithful 28
communication 48
communism 7, 24, 37, 42, 59, 70
communities 1, 4, 8, 15, 20–2
　anarchical society 32
　decolonization 70
　empire 21
　hegemony 80, 104, 108
　justice 43–4
　NGOs 86
　role 109
concert 24, 52, 58–9, 66–8
　core 75
　Europe 70, 82, 98–102, 107
　future 76–9
　hegemony 77
　practice 73–4
confederacy 51, 78, 110–11
Confucius 40
Congress 88
conquest 60
consent 39, 43–4, 59, 89, 107
Constantinople 100
consulates 28, 32
consumers 85
consumption 44, 75
contracts 32, 43, 45, 51
core-periphery system 5, 12–13, 64–79, 95
Corinthians 61, 105–6
corporations 7, 76, 85
Cortez, H. 2
Costa Rica 75
Crete 101
Crimean War 28, 99
Cuba 5, 48, 96
culture 12–13, 37–9, 42, 46, 49
　decolonization 69
　globalization 94
　NGOs 90
　responsibility 2–4

Index

society 31–4
standards 96
unity 15–17
currency 62
Cyprus 101
Cyprus Convention 101
Czech Republic 109

De Gaulle, C. 58
De Vattel, E. 56
debt 62
decentralization 81
decolonization 5–7, 11, 13, 18
  anarchical society 35, 37
  change 92
  future 64, 67–72, 75
  hegemony 109
  integration 47–8, 50, 52
  practice 56, 58
  theory 24
defence 51, 62, 74, 77–8, 110
demand 86
democracy 13, 37, 51, 53, 56
  concert 74
  decolonization 71
  future 76
  NGOs 87–9
  practice 61–2, 84, 90
  standards 95
Denmark 93
dependent states 57, 67, 85, 92, 108
deregulation 77
development agencies 89
diarchy 20, 25, 57, 106, 110
dictatorships 96
dikaion 40–1
dike 40–1, 45
diplomacy 1, 10, 16, 22–4, 28–9
  future 66
  gunboat 86
  justice 39, 42–3, 85
  practice 56, 60, 81
  role 105
  states systems 32
Disraeli, B. 100–1
dissidents 6
distributive justice 38
distributors 42
district commissioners 45
dominion 19–21, 33, 59, 86, 105, 110–11
donors 6–7, 13, 34, 44, 49, 51
  core 72–3, 76
  future 65, 71, 77–8

hegemony 82–3, 110
NGOs 89–91
practice 61–2
proxy 84
resources 74
role 95, 109, 111
Dorr, N. 1
Doyle, M. 93
dual hegemony 20
Dunne, T. 10
dust of empires 58
dustbin of history 92
Dutch 106

East Asia 73, 105, 110
East India Companies 89
East Indians 44
Eastern Crisis 83
Eastern Europe 7, 20, 57
Eastern Rumelia 100
Eban, A. 31
ecology 66
economics 1–2, 6–8, 10, 12–13
  anarchical society 37
  colonization 67–8
  concert 73
  future 64–5, 69, 71, 76–7, 79
  globalization 94–6
  hegemony 105, 108
  integration 46–9, 51–3
  justice 44
  liberalism 80
  liberalization 77
  NGOs 85–9
  policy 78
  practice 57–62
  states systems 27–8, 31–3
  strength 104
  superiority 90
  theory 16, 20, 24
economy 13, 48, 60, 62, 70, 75, 77, 79, 95
Ecuador 57
education 60–1, 68, 70, 77, 86, 95, 99, 108
Egypt 16, 55
élites 33, 44, 47, 62, 68, 70–1, 76, 88
embezzlement 89
empire 19, 21, 23, 42, 55–6, 58
  change 92
  collapse 64
  decolonization 71
  definition 21

hegemony 98, 101, 105, 108
  integration 51–2
Empires 93
England 98–101, 107
English language 100
English School 1, 8, 10, 13, 50
'The English School: An Underexploited Resource in International Relations' 10
environment 13, 37, 75–6, 78–80, 87, 95
envoys 32
equality of states 57–9
ethics 2, 13, 33, 40, 86, 88, 95–6
eurocentrism 5, 11
Europe 2–4, 6–11, 13, 17–21, 25
  Americas 29–30
  collective hegemony 98–9
  Concert 24, 52, 58–9, 66–8, 70, 82, 98–102, 107
  conduct 35
  core 71
  culture 31
  decolonization 69
  economics 48–9
  equality 58–9
  future 78
  hegemony 81, 103, 106–7, 109–10
  integration 47
  international society 32–3, 37, 41, 46
  justice 38, 42
  legitimacy 54, 56
  looking back 66–7
  multiple independences 68
  NGOs 87, 89
  Ottomans 28–9
  responsibility 68
  role 105
  sovereignty 62
  standards 51, 96
  statecraft 78
  states system 15–16, 22–5, 105
  values 34
European Union 4, 72, 78, 110
The Evolution of International Society 5, 11, 51, 54, 81, 92
examples 55–6
Exarchate of Bulgaria 100
executive 38–9
The Expansion of International Society 27, 29, 32, 34, 36, 46, 107
exploitation 109

failed states 12, 64, 66, 71, 78–9, 88, 93
Faithful 28, 39
Festschrift 6
first world 48–9
Florence 104, 106
foreign policy 62
France 16, 23, 28, 36, 67
  future 70, 72
  hegemony 98, 101, 105–6, 110
French Revolution 23
funding 89
future 65–79

Gaza 57
General Assembly 30, 42
genocide 73
Germany 30, 50, 52, 56, 58, 62
  future 72
  hegemony 98, 100–1
  practice 89
Geschichte des Europaeischen Staatensystems 16, 31
ghettos 81
Gladstone, W.E. 99
global society 30–1, 37, 41, 47–8
globalization 6, 10, 13, 64–5
  change 96–7
  economics 94–6
  ethics 88
  future 68, 71, 75, 78–9
  hegemony 108
  practice 80
Golan Heights 57
Gong, G. 51
Gorbachev, M. 20, 37, 49
Gorchakov, A.M. 100
government 50–1, 61–3
grande république 3, 16–17, 23, 28, 32–4, 58, 68, 99, 110
great game 99
great powers 58–9, 61, 65–6
  Europe 98–102
  future 71–3, 76–7, 79
  hegemony 84, 102, 106–7
  practice 80–1, 83, 85
  role 103
greed 87
Greek language 40
Greek Orthodox Church 99
Greeks 3, 15, 18, 23, 33, 40
  change 92
  hegemony 101, 103, 105–6
Grotius, H. 3, 22, 41–2, 45

Index

Group of 77 49
Group of Eight 72
Group of Seven 24, 52, 61, 72
Guises 6
Gulf War 59

Habsburgs 6, 16, 21–3, 28, 47, 55–6, 67, 105–6
Hague Tribunal 29
Haiti 78
Hamburg 58
Harriman, W.A. 30
Hausmacht 21
Heeren, A. 2, 16, 31–2, 34, 36, 61
hegemony 21, 35
  aid 61, 95
  changes 92
  collective 72, 74, 77, 93, 98–102
  concert 77
  core 78
  decolonization 70, 72
  definitions 20, 80–1, 90
  degrees 17–19
  diffused 24
  equality 57–8
  future 65–6, 69, 76, 79
  history 103–11
  integration 47
  intervention 59
  looking back 67
  practice 56, 80–91
  progress 36
  proxy 90
  responsibility 68, 73
  role 94, 103
  rules 55
  sovereignty 62–3
  standards 51–2, 96
  studies 93
  succession 22, 25
Herod, King 21, 55
hierarchy 17, 59, 69
Higgins, R. 12, 22
Hildebrand 38
Hittites 16
Hobbes, T. 2, 38
Holy Alliance 107
Holy Roman Empire 28, 56, 58, 67, 78
Hong Kong 57
Hooker, R. 41
Howard, M. 1
human rights 6, 13, 33, 37
  future 71, 75–7, 79

hegemony 109
integration 47–8, 50–1, 53
NGOs 87–9
practice 56, 59–60, 62–3, 80, 82–4
standards 95
hunter-gatherers 11, 13, 93

immigration 62
imperialism 11, 20–1, 29, 33
  anarchical society 35–7
  change 92
  future 68–9, 71, 75
  hegemony 99, 109, 111
  integration 48, 51
  practice 55, 57, 62, 83–4, 86
  studies 93
independence 19–20, 23–4, 35–7
  absolute 19, 21, 111
  change 92
  concert 74
  decolonization 70–1
  future 64–7, 78–9
  hegemony 81, 84, 106
  integration 51, 53
  justice 38, 43
  limits 82
  multiple 67–71, 80, 82, 86, 104–5, 107
  NGOs 87–8
  Ottomans 100
  practice 56–7, 60, 62–3
  role 107, 109
India 6, 8, 13, 15, 18, 21
  change 96
  future 66, 68–70, 73
  integration 46–7, 49, 51–3
  practice 56
Indochina 25
Indonesia 49, 68, 77
industrial revolution 75
industrial-military complex 89
industrialization 49–50
integration 63, 79, 105, 109–10
interest payments 62
international community 30, 33
International Court of Justice 12
international law 39–40
International Monetary Fund (IMF) 13, 24
  change 94–5
  future 72–3, 78
  hegemony 109
  integration 49, 52
  practice 59, 61

international society 16–17, 19, 22
  anarchical 35–7
  contemporary 56–7
  foundation 42–3
  hegemony 80–91
  integration 46–53
  justice 38
  predictions 64
  relations 1, 14–26
  rules 54–5
  state systems 27–34
international system, changes 92–7
International Systems in World History 5, 8, 11, 93
internet 108
intervention 12, 47–8, 59–60, 63, 76, 82–6, 94–6
invasion 60
Inventing International Society 10
investment 61, 74–6
Iraq 73, 101
Irish Ministry for Foreign Affairs 1
Islam 77, 96
Israel 30, 57, 101
Italy 62, 72, 98, 101, 104, 106

Jackson, R. 71
Japan 13, 30, 32, 50, 52, 58–9
  change 96
  future 66–9, 72–3
  hegemony 105
Judaeo-Christian tradition 41
just war 40, 43
justice 38–45, 60

Kant, I. 2
Karlowitz, Congress of 28
Kazakhstan 77
Keats, J. 2
Kedourie, E. 18
Kennan, G. 6, 65, 99
Khomeini, Ayatollah 34
Kimon 20
King's Peace 23
Klaus, V. 109
Kohl, H. 66
Kosovo 101
Kunz, D. 58
Kurile Islands 57
Kuwait 101

labour 75
Latin 41
Latin America 37

law 2, 12, 19–20, 23, 29, 39–40
  change 93
  future 64, 66, 76–7, 79
  hegemony 104
  integration 46
  practice 55–7, 84, 87
lawyers 12, 22
leadership 6, 12, 22, 48, 52–3, 65, 71
League of Nations 18, 30, 69, 106
Lebanon 57
Legalists 40
legislature 38–9
legitimacy 22–3, 25, 47–8, 50
  change 93
  future 79
  hegemony 107
  integration 52
  practice 54–61, 63, 84
Levant 8, 28
Leviathan state 38, 40, 44
Liberal Party 99
liberalism 44, 50
The Limits of Independence 6–7
linkages 74
Lithuania 110
Little, R. 1, 5, 8, 11–12, 66, 81, 93, 106
living standards 49, 60, 77, 89
Lomé conventions 25, 49
Louis XIV 16, 23, 25, 28, 55–7

Macedonia 101, 105
MacNeice, L. 103
McNeill, W.H. 108
MacNeill, W.H. 81
Manchu Empire 46
Manchuria 44
market 48, 62
Marshall Plan 61
Martin Wight Memorial Lecture 14, 20
Marxism 33, 42, 75
Maurya Empire 18
media 6, 48, 60, 74, 86, 93
mediators 40
Medici family 104, 106
medicine 86, 94, 108
Médicins Sans Frontières 88
Mediterranean 8, 58, 100
Mencius 40
mercantilism 48, 104
Mexico 29
Middle Ages 40
migration 6
Milan 104

military 73, 76, 80, 89, 94, 98–9, 104–5
missionaries 45, 48
Molotov, V. 30, 107
money-making 7
moral obligation 2–3, 8, 12, 50
　future 69, 76
　hegemony 101, 107, 110
　practice 83, 85, 87
Morocco 17, 32, 77
Moslems 39, 101
Mughals 46
multiple independences 67–71, 80, 82, 86, 104–5, 107

Napoleon, Emperor 16, 23, 52, 58, 98, 107, 110
Napoleon III, Emperor 29
Nasser, G.A. 37, 48
nationalism 62, 74, 79, 110
NATO 73
Nehru family 52
Nehru, J. 37, 48–9
neo-colonialism 47, 61, 89
neo-Sumerian responsibility 73
neo-Westphalian system 65–8, 70, 72, 74
Netherlands 28, 105
new world order 50
Non-aligned Movement 30, 37, 48–9, 67
non-combatants 39
non-governmental organizations (NGOs) 8, 80–1, 85–90, 108
non-interference/intervention 67–8, 72–3, 79, 82, 87, 90
Normans 40
North 49–52
North America 68–9
North Korea 73
la Nouvelle Calédonie 57
nuclear weapons 41, 60, 77

Oceania 37, 70
offshore arrangements 75
oil 7, 60, 89–90
oligarchy 104
One World 19
OPEC 49
Orthodox Christians 100
Ottomans 3, 8, 16–17, 23, 28–33, 46, 98–100

Pacific 29, 61, 99, 105

Pakistan 51, 73
Palestine 57, 101
Panama 57
Parma 21
passports 32
Patriarch 100
peace 76–7, 79
peace settlements 20, 22
peacekeeping/making 12, 50, 52, 55
periphery *see* core-periphery system
persecution 6
Persians 3, 20, 23, 25, 32–3, 40, 58, 68
Peru 57
philanthropy 86, 90
Plataea 106
Plato 38
political principle 64
pollution 41
Popes 40
population 41, 44, 57, 60, 76
Porte 28
Portugal 36
post-modernism 64, 71
poverty 6, 60, 95
practice 54–63, 80–91
prisoners 2
private enterprise 67, 75, 79–80, 89, 95–6
private resources 74–5
private sector 8, 13, 109
production 75
profit 7, 13, 67, 86–7, 95–6
progress 36
propaganda 86–7
protectionism 76, 79
Protestants 6, 16, 42
prudence 2, 12, 50, 58, 62, 76
　hegemony 101, 105, 110
　practice 83
Prussia 98
publicity 86
Pufendorf, S. von 14, 16, 38

Qatar 101

racism 68
raison d'état 20, 45, 61, 85
Raj 15, 21
Rana, A.P. 6, 70
reciprocity 16, 31
Red Cross 88
Reformation 6, 41
religion 2, 6, 8, 15, 31, 39
　hegemony 104, 108

justice 42, 48
　practice 55, 59, 86, 88
Republican Party 82
republics 55
res publica 41
resistance 4, 51, 96, 104–5, 109, 111
resource transfers 74–8, 95
responsibility 64, 68, 71–3, 76
　change 95
　hegemony 98, 101, 109
　practice 80, 83, 85, 87
reverse pressures 89–90
The Revolt against the West 36–7
Richelieu, A.J. 45
robber barons 40
Romans 13, 15, 18, 55, 105
Rosenau, J. 81
rules 22, 28–30, 32, 39, 42
　future 68, 72, 76, 78
　hegemony 104, 111
　integration 50
　practice 54–5, 59, 62, 81
Russia 16–17, 25, 48, 50, 57
　empire 64, 71
　future 66–8, 72, 77
　hegemony 98–101, 105, 109
　NGOs 88
　Ottomans 100
　practice 59, 61
Russian language 100
Russian Orthodox Church 99–100
Rwanda 73, 83

St Augustine 39
St Thomas Aquinas 40, 45
San Stefano, Treaty of 100
sanctions 50
Saudi Arabia 57
Saxons 40
Schaumburg–Lippe 21
second world 48–9
Security Council 24, 48, 52, 56, 72, 74, 94
selfishness 50–1
Senegal 48
Senghor, L. 48
settler states 67–8
Sforza 104, 106
Siberia 44
silent disciplining 110
Singapore 57
slave trade 69
social contracts 27
Soeharto, H.M. 52

soft balancing 105
solar system 43, 46, 81, 92, 109–10
South Africa 47
South Asia 6
South East Asia 6
sovereignty 4–5, 7, 19–21, 23
　decline 77–8
　decolonization 71
　erosion 83, 95
　future 65–7, 70
　hegemony 82, 110
　integration 46–7, 51–2, 56–7
　Ottoman 101
　practice 56–7, 60, 62–3, 85, 87
　theory 25
Soviet Union 6–7, 20, 25, 30
　anarchical society 33, 36–7
　collapse 64, 67, 71
　hegemony 107
　justice 43
　NGOs 87
　role 47–9, 51, 57–8, 60, 70
Spaceship Earth 109
Spain 22, 39
Spartans 20, 25, 58, 61, 73, 106
special interest groups 86, 99
Spengler, O. 16
splendid isolation 82
standards 12–13, 33, 37, 51, 60
　future 68, 71, 75–7, 79
　globalization 94, 96
　hegemony 101, 108–9
　NGOs 89–91
　Ottomans 100
　practice 80–2, 84
　role 95
　technology 108
State of the Union address 58
states 2, 4–9, 12–13, 21
　anarchical society 65
　contemporary 56
　control 75
　decline 77–8
　decolonization 72
　democracy 87–9
　dependent 57, 67, 85, 92, 108
　economics 60–2
　equality 57–9
　examples 55
　failed 12, 64, 66, 71, 78–9, 88, 93
　future 65–6
　hegemony 81–4, 103–4, 109
　incompetent 70
　justice 3, 38–45

Index

multiple independences 67–9
NGOs 80–1, 85–91
post-modern 64, 71
role 94
standards 51
types 19–20
states systems 14–21, 25–35
change 92
erosion 97
hegemony 104
integration 46
justice 40–1, 43
practice 81
pressure 105
role 106
The Structure of the International Community 99
sub-Saharan Africa 70, 107–8
Sultans 28
superpowers 25, 60–1, 70, 81, 87
supply 86
supranational executive 39
suzerain system 11, 15, 18–19
anarchical society 35–6
change 92
future 69
hegemony 104, 111
practice 59, 81–2
theory 25
Sweden 30
Switzerland 30
symbols 64, 78
Syracuse 105
Syria 16, 57
De systematibus civitatum 14–18, 23–4, 26
systems spectrum 19–21

Taiwan 30
taxation 44, 73, 86, 88
technology 43, 48, 52, 66, 68–9
change 94–5
future 75–6, 78
hegemony 108
practice 81, 90
role 96
television 50
Tell el Amarna 16
terrorism 94
Thebans 106
theory 54–63
third world 36, 44, 48–9, 56, 71
Thirty Years War 105
Thucydides 61, 73

Tito, J.B. 37, 48
totalitarianism 44
Toynbee, A. 16, 29, 104
trade 8, 13, 20, 28, 49–51, 66–7, 69, 86, 108
trade unions 44, 85–6, 96
trade-offs 74
trading companies 68
tradition 38–9, 41–2, 50, 57, 59
transnational business/enterprise 85–6, 88–90
Treasury 7
treaties 43
tribes 38
Tsars 100, 107
Turkey 4, 28

Ukraine 4
union 34
United Kingdom (UK) 30, 69–70, 107
United Nations (UN) 12, 25, 30–1
anarchical society 36–7
Charter 42, 56, 93, 106
decolonization 72
equality 57
future 65–6, 69–70, 74, 78
integration 48, 50, 52
practice 55, 58
role 94, 107
Secretary General 71
United States (US) 12, 17, 29–30
aloofness 82, 95
anarchical society 37
core 75, 77
future 66–7, 73–4
hegemony 80, 84, 93, 101, 105–7, 109
industrial-military complex 89
integration 46–8, 50
intervention 83
justice 43–4
NGOs 87–8
practice 58–61
responsibility 72
University of Copenhagen 8
University of Virginia 4
usurpation 54–5
Utrecht, Treaty of 23, 28, 45, 54, 105–6

values 3–4, 13, 15, 17, 27, 31
anarchical society 35, 37
future 66, 76
globalization 94

hegemony 107
integration 46, 50
justice 41, 45
NGOs 87
practice 55, 81, 84, 86
role 96
states systems 33–4
technology 108
Venice 7–8, 104, 106
Versailles, Treaty of 20, 69, 105
veto 52, 74
Victoria, Queen 100
Victorians 99
Vienna, Treaty of 20, 23–4, 28, 67–9, 98, 105–6
Vincent, J. 60, 85
visas 44
Voltaire 16, 28, 58

Wade-Gery, R. 1
Wæver, O. 8, 73, 110
warfare 6, 12, 23, 32, 41, 43
  change 94
  future 77
  hegemony 99, 105–6, 110
  integration 48
  practice 56, 58–9, 81
  religion 42
  rules 2, 39–40
Warring States 15, 18, 40
Washington, G. 49
wavelengths 19
weaponry 66
weapons of mass destruction 59, 73, 77
welfare 50, 94, 108–9
Wendt, A. 110
West Africa 5
West Bank 57
Western Europe 40, 66, 73
Western world 6–7
  Cold War 48
  conformity 77
  core 75, 79
  decolonization 71–2
  development 109
  donors 13, 95
  economics 50s
  education 70
  empires 18

governments 2
hegemony 80, 93
international society 36–7
intervention 59–60
justice 42, 44
NGOs 86–9, 91
order 52
scholars 46
standards 12, 51, 84, 96, 108
states systems 15
technology 68
values 33–4
Westphalia, Treaty of 20, 23
  anarchical society 36
  change 92
  Europe 105–6
  future 67
  hegemony 82–5, 105
  integration 46
  NGOs 87
  practice 54–6, 58, 62, 90
  role 94, 107
  states systems 28, 33
  straitjacket 93
Westphalian theory 5–7, 10–13
  anarchical society 37
  future 65–79
  NGOs 86
  role 18
  straitjacket 81
Wight, M. 1–3, 11, 14–26, 35–6, 50, 58, 76, 81, 92–3, 110
Williams, D. 1, 14, 108
Wilson, W. 19, 61
women 37, 82
World Bank 13, 24, 48–9, 51–2, 59, 61, 88–9, 94–6, 109
world empire 108
world government 1, 42, 80
world society 3, 33, 36, 70, 78, 81, 87, 99, 109
World War One 28, 56, 69
World War Two 24, 70, 87, 101

Xenophon 56

Yugoslavia 74

Zheng 106